Praise for
The Glory of a Mustard Seed

Knowing Abeba as a close friend and partner in ministry for the past three decades, I have watched her grow in her identity and Kingdom purpose. Conquering the challenges of culture and language as a Christian businesswoman, Abeba has blossomed in fruitfulness and mastered the mountain of business by her example of love, generosity, and great faith. Leading by example established a model of success for those around her. *The Glory of a Mustard Seed* personifies her life journey. When Jesus said "If you have faith as small as a mustard seed, you can say to this mountain, 'Move from here to there,' and it will move. Nothing will be impossible for you," (Matthew 17:20), He was thinking of Abeba Baughman. She is truly an example of what it means to be so in love with Jesus that everything she encounters becomes a possibility for kingdom advancement. We defeat the enemy by the blood of the Lamb and the word of our testimony. These pages of testimony she has written are an inspiration and example of what it means to grow in faith and be an agent of change in the process.

Dave McDaniel
Men of Issachar Director
Aglow International

Abeba is a dear friend whose life exemplifies the power and truth of the Gospel. Her faith is evident in everything she says and does. Her love for Christ is demonstrated through lovingkindness towards everyone she meets. Jesus said, "Be generous with your lives. By opening up to others, you'll prompt people to open up with God, this generous Father in heaven" (Matthew 5:16 MSG). That describes Abeba. I know her rich testimony and deep spiritual insights will continue to encourage many.

Nancy McDaniel
Global Prayer Director
Aglow Int'l

They overcame by the blood of the lamb and the word of their testimony. That is certainly true for Abeba's testimony of her journey as a young Ethiopian child. Her terrifying journey from a war-torn country to America is a bold testimony of the grace and protection of God for a young woman who escape by walking hours during the night. She left her three children to keep them safe and risked her life to get to America so she could bring them to safety. Over and over God provided special friends who guided her, taught her to cook, and helped her learn her new culture. This book is hard to put down. It is well written and gives an action-packed description of Abeba's story of how God helped her get to America!

Carolyn Suty
Women's Aglow Director for California and Hawaii

"Without faith, it is impossible to please God..." and the Bible tells us that if we even the faith of a mustard seed, we can say to the mountain "be cast into the sea," and the mountain will move.

These Scriptures exemplify AB. As you read her riveting journey from Ethiopia to America, having to leave her children, taking on a false identity to escape with her life, you will see her faith in action from the time she was a small child.

We have been privileged and honored to be spiritual mentors and shepherds to AB. Coming from a mainline denomination, she understood rules, commandments, and what obedience was concerning Father God. What she didn't understand was that Jesus died for her and paid to have an intimate relationship with her.

AB's spiritual growth has elevated her giftings once she learned about her identity in Christ, God's relentless love, and her calling from the Lord. God has used her mightily to serve the broken, the bruised, the abandoned. She is the woman that brings her alabaster box before the feet of Jesus.

Dr. Harlyn and Jeri Matson

the
GLORY
of a
Mustard seed

My Perilous Journey of Faith, Perseverance,
and God's Relentless Love

ABEBA BAUGHMAN

ILLUMIFY
MEDIA.COM

Photo by https://unsplash.com@lauravinck
Cynthia Cutts, Developmental Editor
Deborah Mumma, Assistant Editor

The views and opinions expressed in this book are those of the author and do not necessarily reflect the official policy or position of Illumify Media Global.

Published by
Illumify Media Global
www.IllumifyMedia.com
"Let's bring your book to life!"

Library of Congress Control Number: 2023906435

Paperback ISBN: 978-1-959099-25-3

Cover design by Debbie Lewis

Printed in the United States of America

Dedication

This book is dedicated to Adonai, my Abba Daddy, the God who loves to be involved in all my affairs; who never leaves me nor forsakes me; who walks with me through every desert and swims with me across every river; who carries me when I cannot walk; and who continually forgives me.

To my children, Sara, Elizabeth, Yohannes and Isaac. who because of them I went through the ordeals described in this book. I learned so much through the trials and I learned so much through them.

To my late husband, Clinton, who was master of Agape Love who loved me and my children without condition and without thought of himself.

To my grandchildren, Abraham and Jaden, who fill my heart with joy and keep me young.

To Carolyn Suty, the Aglow S.W. Coastal Director, an anointed Leader of women and men who believes in me.

To my best friend Julia who edifies me and makes me a better person.

To Deanna Worthington who was the first person in my life to cry with me.

To Mary Elizabeth who has always encouraged me and sees me as God sees me.

To ALL my dearly beloved friends who lift my arms towards heaven in prayer, in praise, and worship and those who cry with me on bended knee, and who dance with me and sing with me as we journey toward our Forever Home.

Contents

I tell you the truth, if you have faith as small as a mustard seed, you can say to this mountain, 'Move from here to there' and it will move. Nothing will be impossible for you.

— Matthew 17:20 NIV

Preface

Life is a learning journey. You may travel through a desert, you may stay at home or you may have a career; at all times you are learning. It is your journey.

As I reflect over my life, I've come to realize that God has always been faithful to me. He promised me in His Word that He would enable me to do what He called me to do as part of His perfect plan. I trusted Him for all I needed.

> *All Scripture is inspired by God and beneficial for teaching, for rebuke, for correction, for training in righteousness; so that the man or woman of God may be fully capable, equipped for every good work. (2 Timothy 3:16-17 NASB)*

When I was a child, growing up in Ethiopia I didn't really know God, however I can see now that God knew me. As a young adult I yearned to know God and as I began trusting Him, He became my Lord. My tiny mustard seed faith blossomed into the abiding faith I have today.

This is my story of how God has guided and protected me through the desert storms of my life and how He filled me with His peace.

> *I will give thanks to you, Lord, with all my heart; I will tell of all Your wonderful deeds. (Matthew 7:7 NIV)*

Introduction

Addis Ababa, the capital city of Ethiopia, 1973—I was a fashionable and young single mother of three preschool children living in my war-torn native country of Ethiopia and I had fallen in love with a US Air Force doctor who was employed as a veterinarian. As unusual as this sounds, I had worked with the Americans in my city for many years. Ethiopia had been the main military base for the US in that region of Africa.

We planned to be married. I was excited at the prospect of raising my three children in the United States, the land of freedom and opportunity, safe from the ravages of the current Communist Ethiopian civil war. I was desperate to find a safer place to raise my children. I believed God was leading me to the secure borders of the powerful United States.

The mind of a person plans his way, but the
Lord directs his steps. (Proverbs 16:9 NASB)

In February of 1974 a Communist coup befell Ethiopia and by the spring Ethiopia had broken off military relations with the United States. The Cubans and the Soviet Union took advantage of the situation and both stepped in with massive aid.

The coup was ignited by university students who wanted change; however, they were thwarted by politicians and the government. The military approached the University students and told them "We will help you. We have weapons." There were thousands of political assassinations in Addis Ababa. The military captured the King and put him in jail. Then then they captured the remaining politicians and murdered them all.

The next victims were the educated. As an educated person, I was a target. It was common practice for this new Communist regime to expose the victims of torture on the pavements of the capital city of Ethiopia. More terrifying to me was that children were targets. Reports were announced daily of murdered children; most of them between ages eleven and thirteen. The new military regime felt threatened by anyone who could read or write. Their leader began his own genocide of the generation rising up behind him who might pose a threat. He crowded his opponents into a warehouse, mostly the younger generation, and tear-gassed them.

The bodies of murdered children were piled up in the streets and gutters of Addis Ababa where they were eaten by wild hyenas. The horror was terrifying and is hard to describe as I tearfully write this.

Finding safe refuge for my children was my only focus. Each day as they grew older and more educated, they became a bigger threat to the new Communist reining leaders of Ethiopia.

We had begun processing my fiancé's paperwork so that we could be married. I remember we were at a big party when suddenly there was an announcement and all of the men left. The women stayed, but they were crying. I was the only Ethiopian woman, and I didn't know what was happening. As I mentioned, I had worked with the Americans in my city for many years and Ethiopia had been the main military base for the US in that region of Africa. Now I learned that the Americans were being ordered out of Ethiopia. The man I hoped to marry had three days to leave the country.

PART 1

Leaving Ethiopia

It was impossible for us to be married in three days. All of my American friends and my local friends tried to help me leave Ethiopia with my American doctor. Despite everyone's efforts the paperwork could not be arranged that quickly and fiancé was forced out of Ethiopia without me. He went to Greece and waited for me with hope that I would be able to follow him in the next few days.

I was desperate to take my children out of Ethiopia, so I began making plans to meet my fiancé in Greece. I knew I was being watched so I sent him a 'coded' message, "Your package will arrive soon." He waited in Greece while I planned my escape out of Ethiopia.

I had a cousin living in Djibouti, a tiny French Territory on the eastern side of Ethiopia. I left the capital city seeking a safer plan to leave the region by way of Djibouti. When I arrived at my cousin's house I sent another message to my fiancé, "I am in Djibouti. Your package will arrive soon." What I didn't realize was that it was May Day in Europe, a national holiday, and no messages were being delivered that day.

In May 1973 and 1974 the French government recognized the demands for independence of Djibouti and the Republic of Djibouti was granted. This paved the way for the Somalians to move in and begin killing the Ethiopians who resided in Djibouti. My cousin was concerned for my safety and decided the best thing he could do for me was to send me back home to Addis Ababa in Ethiopia. Residing in Djibouti I was a greater target than back home. Reluctantly I returned back home.

> *Commit to the Lord whatever you do, and*
> *He will establish your plans. (Proverbs 16:3*
> *NIV)*

On May 21, 1974, I received a telephone call from my fiancé, "Happy Birthday, A.B!" he shouted into the phone. "I miss you. What happened to you? Why didn't you come to Greece?"

It was good to hear his voice but my fear of our phone call being overheard caused me to say, "Thank you. You'll get your package soon." It was difficult to talk in secret code without explaining to him what my fears were. "You'll get your package soon. Thank you for calling," I said ending the conversation.

> *A wise person is cautious and turns away*
> *from evil, But a fool is arrogant and care-*
> *less. (Proverbs 14:16 NASB)*

8

The war in Ethiopia continued and I was determined to get my children out of the country. I had divorced their father years before and he was not involved in their lives. Taking them out of Ethiopia was the only way I knew that I could keep them safe as more and more children were killed in my homeland each day. I decided to take the children to Eritrea, the northern part of Ethiopia. My entire family came from Eritrea, and I decided that this was a good place to begin processing my paperwork to go to Greece.

I packed a few bags and took my three children to Eritrea where my uncle helped me enroll my two daughters, Liz and Sara, ages six and seven in an Italian Catholic boarding school. Then I entrusted the care of Yohanas, my three-year-old son, to my uncle and his family. I was careful not to tell anyone where I was going or why for if my leaving was discovered I knew that I would be put in jail. I was equally careful to assure my children that I would return for them. Everything I said was in secret for I did not want to put my children and my family in jeopardy by giving them too much information. It took 21 days to process my plan and now I was ready to go.

I give Almighty God the glory for carrying me through this devastating time in my life. I did not know Him as much as I know Him now. I would send him simple prayers such as "Father God, help me. Protect me and my children. AMEN"

But the Lord is faithful, and He will strengthen and protect you from the evil one. (2 Thessalonians 3:3 NASB)

On the twenty-first day right out of nowhere, I met a woman who suddenly asked "What are you doing here?" Little did I know God was showing up for me as I had prayed. I had been so careful to keep everything a secret, but somehow, I felt I could trust her. "I'm making plans to leave the country and go to America," I told her.

"Wait here," she said. "I know who can help you."

This stranger to me became an instant friend. She introduced me to her Grandpa Joe, an eighty-year-old man who owed her mother a favor. This was God's design demonstrating His mercy and caring. Grandpa Joe was not this man's real name. But even today, I must keep my silence and protect his family from retaliation from those who wanted me dead, so I will continue to refer to him as Grandpa Joe.

"I would be honored to help you," Grandpa Joe said. "Be ready in three days."

"Three days?" I asked. "I'm ready now. Let's go!"

I had visions about my journey of walking on paved streets, jostling a bit on a bus and maybe a little more walking out of Eritrea toward Greece where my American doctor waited with a romantic greeting.

And the LORD will continually guide you,
And satisfy your desire in scorched places,

And give strength to your bones; And you will be like a watered garden, And like a spring of water whose waters do not fail. (Isaiah 58:11 NASB)

"You have three days to pack your stuff," Grandpa Joe kindly explained. "Pack a light bag, pack water to drink, and be ready in three days." He didn't tell me how long it would take to get where we were going, but I was excited that my plan was unfolding.

During those three days I was introduced to two young brothers of the Ethiopian royal family who had run to Eritrea trying to escape assassination. All of the royal family had been arrested and assassinated including the King except for these two college aged boys. They had escaped assassination and were at high risk of being discovered. A friend knew of my plans to leave the country and she also knew these royal brothers. She asked me to help them, and even so I invited these royal family heirs to come along with me on my journey with Grandpa Joe. They gathered a few personal things and packed water to travel with us.

Do nothing from selfishness or empty conceit, but with humility consider one another as more important than yourselves; do not merely look out for your own personal interests, but also, for the interests of others. (Philippians 2:3-4 NASB)

I was astounded when eighty-year-old Grandpa Joe began our trip across the Sahara Desert on foot. Where was my bus I expected? I did not ask out loud. There was no car, just a small band of pedestrians each carrying a small bag! I was carrying a light bag of my belongings and a suitcase with an expensive camera that was very valuable to me but, it became evident that it was not so wise to take it on this trip.

We left Eritrea heading northwest toward the Sahara Desert up hills and down hills. We walked over 10 hours that first day and I discovered that even after all that walking, we were still in Eritrea. My vision of a bus was substituted with the reality of dust and sweat and aching feet as we walked on and on until we finally arrived at our first stop—Keren. We were still in Eritrea, but it was felt so good to stop.

Keren is an agricultural area and we could smell the citrus fruit long before we reached it. I was exhausted, but I became uplifted by the sweet fragrance of the fruit trees as we arrived at this lush, fruitful city. Here we found papayas, oranges, apricots, peaches, and plums.

Grandpa Joe's family members who lived there offered us shelter. We stayed for a few days enjoying the delicious fruits, warm hospitality, and showers with hot running water. Oh, Praise God. Keren was a clean, beautiful, and relatively safe area with plenty of food and water for everyone. For three days I was treated very well and did my best to relax. But on the third day, I was ready to go. The question I asked was, "How many more days?"

I, the Lord, am your God, Who brought you up from the land of Egypt; open your mouth wide and I will fill it. (Psalm 81:10 NASB)

Grandpa Joe looked at me with kind eyes. "Abeba," he spoke to me quietly, "We have seven more days to travel."

Seven More Days

Seven more days!? I was stunned. I assessed my situation and looked around. Here I had my small bag with a few items of clothing and personal things, but I also carried this much larger suitcase with a big camera and lots of photos of my family. This case was heavy. Along with my luggage, I knew I would also have to pack water because the rivers and streams were contaminated with Malaria. I could not carry all this for seven more days!

"Grandpa Joe," I pleaded. "I can't carry all this for seven days. Can we please get a car or use some kind of transportation?"

"It is impossible to use a car," Grandpa Joe shook his head sadly. "The war makes it very unsafe to travel in a car. The roads have been bombed so we can't drive at night. The Guerillas ambush cars and murder the passengers. And no one drives on the roads during the day. Everybody is hiding." The guerrilla fighters hide during the day and ravage at night when they do all their killing when no one can see them.

"Oh," I nodded as I absorbed the information. "We can't take a car, okay. What about a horse? Can we buy a horse?"

Grandpa Joe chuckled. "No horse, but if you don't want to carry your water and luggage we can rent a camel. But my dear, it's very expensive."

"A camel?" I asked. "How expensive?"

"About $40 for the trip," Grandpa Joe explained. I wore my money on my body under my clothes in a little bag. "Yes!" I said. "Please! Please help me rent a camel."

"Okay," Grandpa Joe agreed.

Satisfied that dragging my luggage in one hand and carrying my water in the other hand for seven days had been solved, I pressed Grandpa Joe with more questions.

"Seven days on foot is a long trip," I told him. "Where are we going to sleep?"

"In the fields," Grandpa Joe replied casually, "Or wherever we end up walking to each day. Maybe under a tree or under the stars on the desert sand or in the mountains."

"In the fields? Under the stars?" I asked disbelieving what he was saying. I was an educated city girl, the daughter of a physician. I didn't sleep in the field. "What if there's a snake?" I asked.

"We kill him," Grandpa Joe replied calmly.

"Can I take a bed, so I don't have to sleep on the ground with the snakes?" I begged.

"We'll see what we can do," Grandpa Joe answered patiently.

Do not be anxious about anything, but in everything by prayer and pleading with thanksgiving let your requests be made known to God. (Philippians 4:6 NIV)

A local merchant sold me a rope cot that stood on four legs that was to become my new bed. The legs were stationary so when the camel owner fastened it on top of the camel that I rented, its legs were pointing to the sky.

As we began our seven-day journey I was delighted because I had the camel carrying all my belongings and I only had to walk behind him.

At the start of our journey, there were 11 of us in this group including two little children with their mother, the two royal brothers, Grandpa Joe and 4 other men along with myself. The children's mother and I were the only two women. The children were miserable on the trip and cried and cried. Their mother didn't pack enough water for them and when she ran out of water, she went to the river to fill her water canteens. I knew that Malaria ran rampant through this region and the river water was very contaminated.

On our first day as we crossed the river at Keren, I was horrified to see a human arm and a human head caught in the river rocks beside me. These were terrifying symbols of war. I gasped, shaking and trying not to scream. I kept wondering, "Does his mother know? Did he have a wife? Did he have children? Who will miss him?" I had such mixed emotions. I missed my children whom I left behind in the Italian Catholic boarding school and I was overwhelmed with fear and uncertainty of where I was going.

*Even though I walk through the valley of
the shadow of death, I fear no evil, for You
are with me; Your rod and Your staff, they
comfort me. (Psalm 23:4 NASB)*

God changed me because of this terrifying experience.
This horrible memory causes me to value life even more
than I valued it then. It also made me keenly aware of
how contaminated the rivers were during war. Memories
of that moment swirled around in my head over and over
again for days. But God eventually gave me peace so that
recalling this memory would not cause me to be terror-
ized all over again.

*You will keep him in perfect peace, whose
mind is stayed on You, because he trusts in
You. (Isaiah 26:3 KJV)*

Knowing that the water could be contaminated with
Malaria or Typhoid, I begged the children's mother not to
give the children poisoned river water, and instead gave
her water from my supply. She gratefully accepted and
in no time, I was out of my water supply. Walking in the
heat for 10 to 12 hours without water was a fierce challenge, but I decided it was better than having the children
die along the trail from drinking the putrid river water.
The rest of the group laughed at me for refusing to drink
the river water.

Do not withhold good from those to whom
it is due, When it is in your power to do it.
(Proverbs 3:27 NASB)

On the first night of this seven-day journey we slept under the night sky. I remember laying on my rope cot and counting stars. The mother, her little children and I slept in the middle of a circle of men who protected us. Praise Jesus! I saw God's protection in this like a wall of fire surrounding me.

> *For I, saith the LORD, will be unto her a wall*
> *of fire round about, and will be the Glory in*
> *the midst of her. (Zechariah 2:5 KJV)*

The next day we walked about 12 hours and found rest in the home of another of Grandpa Joe's acquaintances. He knew everybody because he is the father of many Guerilla fighters. As I lay there on my cot I wondered about where God was taking me.

> *We know that all things work together for*
> *good to them that love God, to them who*
> *are the called according to His purpose.*
> *(Romans 8:28 KJV)*

Each day it was the same, quietly walking along the trail hoping for a welcoming breeze. Since I hadn't known we would be walking the whole trip I was not prepared with walking shoes. My feet were sore, blistered and aching with every step. I suffered the permanent loss of one of my toenails from walking this desert trip with wrong shoes. A minor scar compared to the emotional impact this journey continues to have on me.

Because we were heading toward the mountains, we were somewhat protected usually avoiding the wind when it came up strong against us. We were always alert and watching for any signs to keep us from becoming victims of the war. We walked from village to village from Keren on to Akordat and then to Tessenei. Our fear for our lives was greatest at night. In the day when we would hear bomber planes, we would duck and hide.

The war that was raging was not face-to-face combat; it was Guerilla fighting. The soldiers would come out of the bushes and ambush their enemies. An attack was a very real possibility for our little band of travelers. Grandpa Joe had a plan for us in case we were caught. He told us to lie about where we were headed and why.

"If anyone in our group is ever stopped by the Guerillas," Grandpa Joe stressed, "Tell them we are going to a big wedding in Sudan."

The Arrest

It was day three of our journey when suddenly as we walked along the road the Guerilla fighters jumped out from the bushes and surrounded us at gunpoint.

"Where are you going?" the leader demanded.

Grandpa Joe spoke up, "We are going to a big wedding in Sudan. We have family there and we want to celebrate with all of our family."

The soldiers began scavenging through our luggage. They ransacked every bag, but seemed to accept our lie about going to the wedding—until they got to my camera bag. Inside they found my camera with several lenses and rolls of undeveloped film. They accused me of being a war correspondent taking pictures of the war.

"What is this?" they grabbed my camera and examined it carefully. "You are not going to a wedding. You are CIA."

"I am not CIA," I cried. "I'm just going to the wedding to take pictures."

The leader did not believe me.

"All can go but her," the leader said, pointing at me. Grandpa Joe and the rest were told to continue because

they knew Grandpa Joe. "She is CIA. She comes with us."
I was terrified and scared for my life.

> *Do not fear, for I am with you; Do not be*
> *afraid, for I am your God. I will strengthen*
> *you; I will also help you, I will also uphold*
> *you with My righteous right hand.' (Isaiah*
> *41:10 NASB)*

They took me to a private home and held me prisoner. It wasn't an actual jail, just a home where I was fed a regular meal. I had been eating dried fruit, beef jerky and crackers so the meal was a relief. I told them over and over that I was not CIA.

"I'm going to a wedding!" I insisted. "I'm taking my camera to the wedding. Please just develop the film you've found. It's family. I'm supposed to take pictures of the wedding!"

I was terrified. They were suspicious of me because I came from the capital city of Ethiopia, Addis Ababa. The current government of Ethiopia would not allow anyone to leave the country so my captors were suspicious as to why I was allowed to leave. Everyone was expected to stay and fight in the war. Before I began this journey, many people had been held in prison or killed for trying to leave Ethiopia. I feared that I was going to be one more casualty of war.

The soldiers didn't mistreat me, but they continued to insist that my camera was evidence that I was not who

I said I was. My fellow travelers were waiting outside the home we had previously stayed the night before, not moving on without me. I was comforted by their resolve to stick together. It would have been much simpler for them to have abandoned me and left me to the Guerillas. While I was being held prisoner, Grandpa Joe sent a message to his sons, many who were Guerilla fighters.

Finally I spoke very boldly to them. I said to my captors, "Listen, I am from the Hamasaid tribe." This was my family's native tribunal connection, and they recognized the tribal name. "You must let me go to the wedding! My traveling companions are not leaving without me!" I insisted that they not stall our travel plans anymore. Since they were being aggressive with me, I felt I needed to boldly speak what Grandpa Joe said to say even though it pains my spirit to lie.

I demanded "Send me to the wedding or send me home!" standing up to these men with guns.

> *Be strong and courageous, do not be afraid or in dread of them, for the Lord your God is the One who is going with you. (Deuteronomy 31:6 NASB)*

He will not desert you or abandon you."

At last, a message returned from one of Grandpa Joe's sons. I don't know what it said, but the Guerilla fighters let me go and we were on our way. They confiscated my camera, film, and suitcase, but they released me unharmed. Once again, my Almighty God who watches over me stepped in and rescued me.

> *They will fight against you, but they shall not prevail against you. For I am with you,"* *says the Lord, "to deliver you." (Jeremiah 1:19 NKJV)*

The Blue Nile River Gorge

After sitting for so long under house arrest, Grandpa Joe and my other traveling companions were concerned about my getting up and walking for long hours again.

"I think it could cause you problems to walk all day after sitting for such a long time," Grandpa Joe said. "You will have to ride the camel." All I could think about was 'I'm FREE!' I did not care if I rode a camel, a horse or a cow.

"But what about all my things?" I asked, looking at my remaining suitcase, water and bed.

"You must leave the bed," Grandpa Joe said.

Reluctantly I had to give up my bed. I got on the camel and began another day of travel. I sat between the camel's two humps and was so thankful to be moving on.

Praise the Lord! Oh, give thanks to the Lord,
for He is good; For His mercy is everlasting.
(Psalm 106:1 NASB)

We came to the Blue Nile River Gorge where Grandpa Joe explained we had to cross to get to our destination.

He gave us careful instructions on how to cross. This is the water source for all Egypt. Sometimes the water gushes and sometimes it doesn't, and Grandpa Joe had to gauge the safest time to cross over.

"Walk fast, otherwise the water gush will come and sweep you off your feet." Grandpa Joe was stern as he explained the order of how we would cross and what to expect. I broke off from the group for a few minutes and prayed, "Father God, help us, AMEN."

> *For I, the Lord your God, will hold your right hand, saying to you, "Fear not, I will help you." (Isaiah 41:13 NKJV)*

It took us 20 minutes to cross the Blue Nile River Gorge. We walked diagonally upstream across the river feeling the current swirl around our legs and powerfully push us back down stream. The men carried the children on their neck and shoulders. The water was cold coming up all the way to my waist. I could hear a loud hum from the strong current. I remembered the dismembered bodies I'd seen in the river at Keren and prayed that the children would be spared seeing body parts rushing down the river.

Finally, we were on the other side and with trembling legs we all collapsed on the riverbank. We were so tired from fighting against the current. We fell into lush green foliage, mud, and rocks and rested. It felt so good to look at the river and see the other side.

Suddenly, we heard a rushing sound. It sounded like rain, but it wasn't raining. It got louder and sounded like it was raining hard. The next second a flash flood tumbled down the river and the water level rose six to eight feet. We scrambled off that riverbank for higher ground and then looked back. I gasped at the close call we had just experienced and I remembered my prayer before we began to cross this stream. I looked to heaven. "Father, how powerful are You?" I asked the heavens. I was absolutely amazed at the safety God had provided.

> *But Jesus answered and said to them, "You are mistaken, since you do not understand the Scriptures nor the Power of God." (Matthew 22:29 NASB)*

The Long Night

That night, as I slept on the ground with my head on my suitcase, I realized how my faith was growing. I had so many doubts, so many worries about my children left behind, yet I was beginning to trust that God was watching over all of us. I watched the mother in our party with her two children and I asked myself, "Why didn't I bring my children with me?" It was God who saved them from this trial. The reason was simple. I was afraid of the unknown, the war, the violence and what tragedy might happen along the way. God had wisely placed them out of harm's way.

> *Therefore there is now no condemnation at all for those who are in Christ Jesus. (Romans 8:1 NASB)*

Laying down that night, I was comforted knowing that for the moment my children were safe. I still wondered if I had done something wrong by not bringing them with me. My prayer was two-fold that night. Reflecting over the tragedy averted at the river I prayed, "Father God, help my children and help me. Amen."

That if our heart condemns us, that God is greater than our heart, and He knows all things. (1 John 3:20 NASB)

It was a dark, lonely hour before I fell asleep. I wondered if I was at the beginning of the end of everything. I was tired, desperate, overwhelmed and extremely discouraged. I was not afraid of going forward because God was with me to give me courage.

Wait for the Lord; Be strong and let your heart take courage; Yes, wait for the Lord. (Psalm 27:14 NASB)

My thoughts wandered to 1974 when I was young, twenty-eight years old. I pondered how in Ethiopia my upbringing made me courageous. We learn courage from our parents at an early age because of our culture. My parents taught me how to survive in every situation. Although my father died before I turned twelve, he started teaching me as if I was grownup when I was just eight years old. He taught me how to solve problems. I learned to take care of his patients who came to our Medical Clinic. We also had a milk farm and I helped him sell milk to the local people which included native Ethiopians, Indians, Italians, and many others. We were known for having good milk so many came to buy.

Still resisting sleep, my thoughts turned back to my current situation. I was afraid of the unknown. Even though I had seen God's powerful answer to my prayer at the river, nagging doubts surfaced as I struggled to drift off to sleep. "What if my plan doesn't work? How will I get my children?" I was so emotional because it was a grueling journey. "When I get to Greece what if I find out my American doctor is already married? What if I'm stuck and I can't reach my kids?" Today my 'God of Many Chances' has taught me that even if I do not take the straight and narrow path into His arms, He is still waiting for me with His unfailing grace. He is guiding me toward Him even when I get off the trail. He is waiting at the Fork.

In all your ways acknowledge Him, And He will make your paths straight. (Proverbs 3:6 NASB)

"Father God," I prayed, "I know You are with me, that You are by my side each day. But when are we getting there and how hard will it be to get there?"

Alone on the Trail

Early the next morning, our small band of travelers set out after a good night's rest. Bathroom breaks were just wherever we could find a bush. The men were very protective and watched out for us. When we slept under the stars, they put us in the middle and slept in a circle around us. They didn't carry my belongings, but they gladly carried river water for those who would drink it.

Grandpa Joe was cheery this morning. "AB," he said. "The next place we stay, you will drink milk."

I was so excited. It had been a while since I'd had such a treat and I looked forward to fresh milk with every step of the day's journey.

When we arrived at the home of another friend of Grandpa Joe's, timidly I asked my host if she would boil the milk before she served it. I watched the servant wash the glass before she poured the milk. Humoring me, my gracious host accommodated my request to boil the milk. I was so concerned about contracting Malaria or some other disease that might be lurking in this remote area. After the milk had boiled, I watched as she poured it into the clean glass. But the milk didn't look right. It was dark and very thick.

"Oh my!" I exclaimed. "It's so thick!" My family owned a dairy. I knew what fresh milk should look like and I knew this wasn't right.

"What do you feed your cows here on the desert?" I asked.

"Oh, you city people!" exclaimed my host. "You never get this kind of milk in the city. This is camel milk!"

Instantly I wasn't hungry for milk anymore. "Oh, no thank you," I said. "I don't think I want milk after all." I was embarrassed and thought they must think I was so dumb.

I had been looking forward to drinking that milk all day. I had been so excited, and now I wanted to cry. I asked my hostess to boil some water and she made me some tea. Then I paid my her two dollars to boil enough water to carry me through to the next stop.

Give thanks to the Lord, for He is good; For His mercy is everlasting. (Psalm 118:1 NASB)

Throughout our seven-day journey we could see a mountain ahead. Grandpa Joe kept telling me, "When we reach the top of the mountain we're almost there." But he'd been saying that for days and we didn't seem to be getting any closer.

In defiance I announced, "I'm not looking at that mountain anymore!"

What I didn't realize then is that the mountain in that memory was a metaphor for all of life's challenges. I've learned that God is the owner of all mountains in life; all problems, goals, or things we desire. He is not too far away. In fact, He's right within reach. I just have to surrender to Him and by my faith God will move the mountain toward me.

> *And Jesus said unto them, Because of your unbelief: for verily I say unto you, If ye have faith as a grain of mustard seed, ye shall say unto this mountain, Remove hence to yonder place; and it shall remove; and nothing shall be impossible unto you. (Matthew 17:20 KJV)*

The next day, we ventured on to an open area, which was straight and not hilly or rough terrain. It was much easier walking and our group just walked and walked. It was here that we saw hundreds of camels lined up in a single line.

We could see the camels from a distance. I noticed something shiny in the sky and pointed at it. "What is that little thing?"

"Hide!" Grandpa Joe called to us and pointed toward the brush alongside the trail.

I looked up and realized that what I had seen in the sky was a Bomber, a military combat aircraft designed to attack ground targets, and if we were spotted, we might be shot. The plane flew by, and we continued on our way getting closer to the camel caravan. I was amazed when I saw the Bomber come back and the camels began lying down from the front of the row to the back, one after the other in succession, just like dominos! And then on their knees, the camels continued to move forward crawling on the dirt.

"They are trained for war," Grandpa Joe explained. "They carry supplies for the Guerrilla fighters. When they hear an airplane and they are in an open field they know to get down but continue on." I was fascinated by the camels as they continued to lie down one after the other and then crawl along the ground.

Our journey continued, but I was keenly aware that the war was going on all around us. I hadn't seen a car for days. Here all the cars were hidden during the day for if a Bomber pilot would see a car, it would be blown up. Sometimes, when we reached a city or a little village, we might see a car late in the afternoon.

No weapon that is formed against you will succeed. (Isaiah 54:17a NASB)

These days blended together in my mind. Some days were smooth and I could rest some place. Other days were more exciting and after traveling on foot for 10 to 12 hours, I would simply crash to sleep on the barren ground. Bathing was a luxury we no longer experienced. We ate crackers and grain.

Despite the hardships, sometimes we would find a hut to stay in. I recall that the people were very helpful. They were in trouble themselves, yet even in a struggling economy they shared what they had to help us.

I marveled at the tenacity of Grandpa Joe. At 80 years old, he was the strongest man I had ever met in my life. He walked and directed us every day. Along the trail he explained that his sons were fighting in the war. We were walking towards Sudan where Grandpa Joe and his family lived. He picked up his retirement check every year in Eritrea where I met him and then he would return to Sudan where his wife and daughters waited eagerly for him.

We neared the border of Sudan towards a city named Kasala. Grandpa Joe encouraged us to walk extra miles that day because in Kasala we would be hosted by his friends. There would be beds, clean water, showers and good food. Around midnight we arrived and I fell asleep to Grandpa Joe's comforting words.

"Don't worry about Bombers," Grandpa Joe said. "They won't bomb the city."

The next morning the mother and her two children left our small band, but the rest of us stayed together. We were staying in the home of a Muslim family. I had been raised to believe that it was unholy to eat food prepared by anyone Muslim or in a Muslim home. So, when meals were served, I had a very hard time trying to eat food in this house.

Grandpa Joe said, "Bless the food before you eat and then you will be okay." At that time on my spiritual journey, I did not understand this.

It's not what goes into your body that defiles you; you are defiled by what comes from your heart. (Mark 7:15 NLT)

As hungry as I was, for a few days I had a hard time eating anything but dry bread.

"The meat is unholy," I told Grandpa Joe.

Grandpa Joe understood but encouraged me. "You need to eat."

I struggled. My fears were based on my culture, so I prayed and asked God to bless the food. With resolve I told myself, "Forget it, I'm just going to eat it!"

I took a bit of roasted chicken and with that first swallow I thought I was going to get sick. Oh, my gosh! It was so hard! But, once I swallowed it, I was okay.

In everything give thanks: for this is the will of God in Christ Jesus concerning you. (1 Thessalonians 5:18 KJV)

Planning for Khartoum

I began planning as we were on our way to Khartoum, the capital city of Sudan, which is located on the confluence of the Blue Nile and White Nile rivers. Grandpa Joe finally arriving home, stayed with his wife and children. The men and I continued our journey. We were free to travel; no more camels and walking for days and bad water. I alone continued with the men. The culture is very different there than it is in the United States where women are considered as sex objects. I had no concern for that sort of thing. The men were my protectors. Besides, two of the men were from the royal family and they would not let any harm come to me if they could help it.

The first thing we had to do was to register as refugees. With that completed it took us six days to get Passports, vaccines, and begin our travel plans. During this time, we rented a place. We had one room where we all slept in a tiny house. The men gave me the only bed and they all slept on the floor. They were not drinkers and they smoked outside out of respect for me.

*Be strong and courageous, do not be afraid
or in dread of them, for the LORD your God
is the One who is going with you. He will not
desert you or abandon you. (Deuteronomy
31:6 NASB)*

When everything was officially processed for travel outside of the country, I was surprised that I did not receive a Passport. Instead, the six of us received one document with all six of our names on it. It was written in Arabic, and none of us could read it. It wasn't a good sign, but I pushed aside my fears, because at least now we were going! Individually we should have had separate documents.

*The Lord keeps you from all harm and
watches over your life. The Lord keeps watch
over you as you come and go, both now and
forever. (Psalm 121:7-8 NLT)*

On the way to Khartoum

Just as we were about to leave for Khartoum, I met a Christian man, a citizen of Sudan, whose main business was laundry. He heard of our plan to leave the country and about our long journey over the Sahara Desert. He felt sorry for us, so he brought us food and after a brief visit, he took us to his house and introduced us to his family. He was very eager to help us.

The traveling document that we had which included all of our names on the same paper was what we planned to use in Khartoum. That was going to be a difficult task. The Sudanese Security would most likely challenge our processing papers.

Our host's wife took me aside, "AB," she said taking my hand, "You cannot go on this trip dressed like you are."

I looked down at my clothes. I was clean and attractively dressed in American fashion. "Why not?" I asked.

"You are going to travel dressed like the Sudanese," she insisted. "This paper is no good. If they catch you, the military Security will put you in jail." I knew that God was watching out for me.

The Lord keeps watch over you as you come and go, both now and forever. (Psalm 121:8 NLT)

There was deep concern in her voice and her eyes sparkled as she went on. "I'm going to dress you like a Sudanese," she smiled. She brought out a beautiful yellow costume like native Sudanese women wore. She wrapped me up in this bright flowing gown and covered my head in a hijab. It was beautiful. As I got on the bus to go on to Khartoum, I know that she and her husband prayed for my safe passage.

I sat next to a window in the bus and looked across at the others in my party. I wasn't sure if they believed in God the same as I did. I wasn't sure if they had the same faith that I had. I looked at the two young men of the royal family so tormented. They had been thrown away by their country and their people because after the King was killed, they were targets for violence as well. These young people had no choice but to try to escape. I wrapped my fingers around the little New Testament Bible that I carried with me and hoped that the passages I'd read to them each day had touched their hearts. The bus bumped along the road and I looked out the window wondering where God was taking me and prayed.

You can make many plans, but the Lord's purpose will prevail. (Proverbs 19:21 NLT)

We rounded a corner on a narrow road and the bus slowed down to a crawl when all of a sudden military Security Guards jumped on the bus with guns pointed and stopped the bus.

"All those who are not citizens of Sudan, get down OUT OF THE BUS!" the guard shouted. My companions were solemn as they filed off the bus. My name was on their documents and I was not a citizen of Sudan but, I was dressed in that yellow Sudanese costume and hijab. It was as if Someone told me to stay. I prayed for them "My trust is in You, God, and I give thanks to You for Your love and protection. In Jesus' name, Amen."

So, I remained on the bus. I sat in my seat, looking out the window. I started praying more trying to remain calm as all the people from the bus lined up to have their papers inspected.

"Father God, help me," I begged silently. "Comfort them. Help them." I could hear my own heartbeat and focused on breathing normally. I was so frightened.

There were a lot of non-citizens lined up waiting for Security to check documents. One by one the guards looked over the paperwork at gunpoint. I shuddered. Once the guards had looked at my traveling companions' paperwork, I knew we would be jailed or killed.

Finally, with only one person ahead of the men from my traveling party to go, our bus driver began ranting and raving and acting weird.

"I'm leaving!" he shouted suddenly waving his hands. He jumped out of his driver's seat and began shouting out the door. "I have to go! I have to go! I'm leaving! I'm leaving. There is no time for this!" He was acting so crazy, and the guards were clearly alarmed. I tried to remain calm, but my heart was beating frantically.

I held my breath. This could be very bad because Security had no reason to listen to this bus driver.

The Security Guard handed a paper back to the man ahead of my companions without looking at it and said, "Go." I knew God had moved His hand.

> *In my desperation I prayed, and the Lord listened; He saved me from all my troubles. (Psalm 34:6 NLT)*

And just like that, the guard let my group back on the bus. He allowed one guy before my group and my entire group, including the royal brothers, to get back on the bus.

Retelling this today, I still experience chills. For when that happened, I knew without a doubt that they were released because of God's mercy on us. That memory inspires me still today.

> *Therefore let's approach the throne of grace with confidence, so that we may receive mercy and find grace for help at the time of our need. (Hebrews 4:16 NASB)*

As the bus rumbled on down the road, I sat still in my window seat marveling at how the hand of God had worked with the bus driver and the Security Guard. It was late in the afternoon and the sun was descending gently over the desert with bright orange and red streaks. I looked toward heaven and whispered, "Thank you, Father, for protecting us today."

Then I thought about what lay ahead and I prayed, "Father God, just help me." I don't know what religion that bus driver was or why God chose to use him that day, but I took great comfort in knowing that the laundry man and his wife had been praying for me and that the bus driver's quick thinking had truly saved all of us. I pulled the yellow hijab around me and marveled at my friend's wisdom in insisting that I dress as a Sudanese.

Arriving in Khartoum

It was dark when we came to Khartoum where everybody but me had a family to stay with. As we began to split up everyone was anxious to get to their destinations and I suddenly realized that I didn't know what was going to happen to me that night. I had a cousin in Khartoum who had lived here for eight months with her husband. I knew I could stay with her, but first I would have to find her. It was too late to begin looking for her on this night and Sudan was fire hot.

"You can't leave me here," I implored them at the bus stop. "Please, you must take me to a hotel."

So, my traveling companions agreed to take me to a hotel. I didn't know much about the hotel system in Sudan, but I told them that I needed to conserve my funds and that I didn't want to pay too much.

The first place they took me to was a dormitory style inn. It was just a big room which had three rows of ten beds each.

"This won't do!" I insisted.

"Well, you said you wanted inexpensive," was the reply.

From there they took me to a grand hotel that was lavish and extremely expensive. I told them that hotel was not suitable either.

My third choice was a hotel that offered rooms, but there were three beds to a room, and I would have two unknown roommates.

I looked into the room they showed me and there was no one there. In my head I was thinking, "What happens if two guys show up in the night?" But it was late and hot and I was extremely tired. Fortified by my fortunate experience on the bus, I suddenly felt like it was safe to take this room. It was as if a voice from heaven said, "Take it!"

I thanked my group, booked the room and went to bed. I slept throughout the night and no one showed up during the night as a roommate. "Thank You, Father."

When you lie down, you will not be afraid;
When you lie down, your sleep will be sweet.
(Proverbs 3:24 NASB)

PART 2

Do You Know my Cousin?

The next morning was my big test. Khartoum is a huge city and here I discovered that nobody spoke English. I got up, bathed, dressed in my long pants and shirt. I checked out of the hotel and then decided to find my cousin Asklu. She didn't know that I was coming and I didn't have an address for her. I counted on God to help me.

> The LORD says, "I will rescue those who love me. I will protect those who trust in My name. [15] When they call on Me, I will answer; I will be with them in trouble. I will rescue and honor them. (Psalm 91:14-15 NLT)

I wrote words on a note pad and then hired a taxi to take me to an Ethiopian community in Khartoum. The taxi driver spoke a little bit of English and he drove me to the community I requested and stopped at an Ethiopian restaurant. I was so happy. I thought, "I'm going to find my cousin now!"

I sat down outside the restaurant with a photo of Ask-lu and her husband. All day I sat there showing the photo and asking if anyone knew my cousin and her husband.

Several people responded, "Yes, I know them," and "No, I don't know where they live." This was very discouraging, but I tried to remain hopeful.

Finally, another taxi driver came by. "Please sir, do you know my cousin?" I asked, showing him the photo.

"Yeah, I know them," he replied. "

Do you know where they live? I must find them," I asked.

"Sure, I know where they live," he replied.

"Will you take me?" I asked.

"For forty dollars," he said.

It was deathly hot sitting there. I was dripping with sweat. This was the kind of heat that people die from. I was so discouraged as I had no clue how to find my cousin without his help. Sitting in the sun wearing my long pants and heavy shirt, I was desperate to find Asklu.

"Wait here," I told him.

I went into the restaurant where I bought a lighter shirt and a jihab style scarf to drape over me. And then the man and I got into his taxi, and we drove up and down, up and down, up and down all the streets trying to find my cousin's house.

I was devastated. The taxi driver couldn't remember which house belonged to Asklu and her husband. And it was no wonder since all the houses in this community looked exactly the same.

The driver spoke Sudanese and Arabic and we had a difficult time communicating. I was so disheartened. The scorching heat beat down on the taxi and with no air conditioner, it was unbearably hot.

Finally, he stopped the car and I got out of the taxi. I was getting scared that I would never find Asklu. The tears were brimming in my eyes, and I was extremely tired from the stress of traveling in such uncertainty.

The taxi driver then took me to a place where a water pot was buried in the ground. Every so many feet a water pot was buried for public use, otherwise people would die on the street from thirst. Then he left. I got a drink of water with the dipper, wiped my brow and I looked around at the unfamiliar neighborhood. I decided on a direction and began walking again. I wasn't really sure what I was looking for anymore. I just needed to find Asklu.

I was walking slowly as the late afternoon turned to dusk. I was incredibly tired, soaked with sweat and discouraged. The air had cooled a bit and people were beginning to come out to walk to the Market where people danced to music and families bought food from street vendors. I looked down the street and saw a woman with two boys. I turned and began walking the other way.

Then I heard the woman say, "That girl looks like my cousin, AB." As I looked back, the boys shook their heads, but I heard her insist, "No, I really believe that's AB."

I turned around and it was Asklu! I was so happy to find her. We cried and cried, hugging in the street. Finally, we went to her house where I met her husband.

The Lord is my Strength and my Shield;
My heart trusted in Him, and I am helped;
Therefore, my heart greatly rejoices, and with
my song I will praise Him. (Psalm 28:7 NASB)

I was surprised to learn that everybody slept outside in a bed at their house. I was so happy to be staying with my cousin and her family. I felt comfortable and safe. The whole family welcomed me and began helping me prepare the long, tedious process of obtaining a Passport to travel to the United States.

I stayed in Sudan for eighty-one days. It seemed like forever! That was a record for me to wait for something. Everyone who came to Sudan to get a Passport usually had to stay five to six years before all the final processing was completed. This included standing in line and competing for the proper paperwork day after day. God provided yet another miracle of friendship to expedite my travel.

The first action in my plan was to send a telegram to my American fiancé.

"I'm in Khartoum—stop—Send plane ticket from Khartoum to US—stop—AB." This was a critical piece of obtaining a Passport. I had to be able to prove how I would leave the country.

My fiancé sent a plane ticket in my name to the Swiss airlines. When I went to pick it up, I was surprised to recognize the young man who worked at the ticket counter; another God encounter. This young ticket agent had worked for the Ethiopian airlines in Addis Abeba and I used to invite him to our home for family gatherings.

"What are you doing here?" I asked him.

"Never mind that!" he said. "What are you doing here?"

I explained that I was here to obtain a Passport and planned to marry an American doctor in the United States.

My ticket agent friend replied, "I'm going to take you to my family. My mother will want to prepare a dinner for you. AB, I'll help you get your Passport."

And my God will supply all your needs According to His riches in glory in Christ Jesus. (Philippians 4:19 NASB)

When I went to dinner with his family, I discovered that obtaining a Passport here in Khartoum was going to be a challenge. The system was extremely slow. Immigration officials accepted about twenty-five people per day and it didn't matter how long you had been waiting in the line, when the officials decided they were finished for the day, they closed up. I was astonished to learn that people would often stand in line day after day and month after month, year after year, sometimes getting up as early as 2 a.m. to be the first in line at the Immigration Office. It was common for refugees to take five or six years to obtain a Passport. How long would it take for me to acquire my Passport?

My ticket agent friend was eager to help me. He took a piece of paper and wrote a note with a person's name on it.

"Take this to the immigration building tomorrow," he said as he handed me the note. I looked at the note, it was written in Arabic, but the name on the note was written in my language. "Take this to the side gate and give it to the guard. Don't go to the refugee line." My friend said. "My mother will dress you as the Sudanese."

"Oh!" I exclaimed. "I have a Sudanese costume from another friend."

"Good," my friend replied. "Wear that and go to the side gate. Do not get in the refuge line."

Well, the next morning, I dressed in my beautiful yellow dress and hijab and set out for the immigration office. There were hundreds of refuges waiting in line outside the building to get a Passport. The line was the full length of the building on two sides. My heart sank thinking how terrible it would be to stand in the Sudan heat waiting in that line for days AND YEARS.

I walked across the street from the line to the side gate. I met the guard at the gate and gave him my note. He took the note, read it, looked me in the eye and said, "Go."

I will give him the key to the house of David—
the highest position in the royal court. When
he opens doors, no one will be able to close

INTRODUCTION

*them; when he closes doors, no one will be
able to open them. (Isaiah 22:22 NLT)*

I opened the gate, went on into the building and within hours it was done. I had a Passport to travel to the
United States.

Next Stop — Cairo

When my American friends were forced to leave Ethiopia, they became scattered around Europe. While I waited in Khartoum with my cousin, Asklu, letters began arriving from my American friends. My fiancé sent my address in Khartoum to my friends, and they wrote me letters inviting me to stay with them when I left Sudan. I was encouraged by the invitations I received from Nepal, Greece, Italy, and Cairo. My friends remembered me and were offering their help and support.

My fiancé arranged my ticket for Cairo since it was the closest to Sudan. I boarded a Swiss Airlines plane to Cairo where I could stay with my dear friend Judy and her husband, Dr. Watson. Dr. Watson was an American physician and he had been my fiancé's boss in Ethiopia. I had spent a lot of time with Judy and her husband, and we were very close friends. From the Watson's home, my fiancé and I would travel to the United States. My plan was finally taking shape and I was beginning to see God's plan unfolding before me.

When I arrived in Cairo, I was dressed the way I dressed back home in Ethiopia. I was a city girl with my own style and fashion sense, and I had planned for this trip. I had on a stylish peach colored, two-piece outfit with short-sleeve jacket and slacks. It was beautiful. Airport security was extremely tight in Cairo and Judy was not allowed entrance to greet me. So, she sent her Egyptian driver to the gate. When I stepped off the plane, he was standing there holding a sign with my name on it. He had a note from Judy which said, "We don't live too far away from the airport. Think of what you are most hungry for. That's what we'll have to eat when we get home."

When the driver brought me out to the car where Judy was waiting, she was shocked at my appearance.

"AB!" she cried, hugging me and then pushing me back to look at me. She hugged me again. "You look beautiful. I thought you would look like a ragged refugee, but you look good! You look really good!" She hugged me again and we cried joyful tears of celebration.

"What do you want to eat?" Judy asked as we settled into the car to travel to her home.

"Milk and eggs," I replied with conviction. It had been so long since I'd had either and I was craving both.

> *Even strong young lions sometimes go hungry, but those who trust in the LORD will lack no good thing. (Psalm 34:10 NLT)*

The driver started Judy's car and we drove a few miles from the airport to Judy's home. It was a beautiful Egyptian mansion. After months of traveling across the desert with dust and dirt and unbearable heat, it was so awesome to be in a house with cool air conditioning, clean beds, safe food to eat, and Judy's children joyfully playing in the house. I relaxed and thanked God for the blessing of good friends and their warm hospitality. That first night Judy bought gallons of milk and dozens of eggs. After about one cup of milk and a few scrambled eggs, my cravings were over. I felt like myself again.

Except for my hair. My natural hair is very kinky and curly, and I preferred to straighten it and style it fashionably. I remember the laughter when Judy's children decided to try to take the kinkiness out of my hair as I waited for my fiancé to arrive.

Within a few days, my fiancé arrived. When I embraced him at the airport, he folded me into a big hug and I sobbed into his shoulder. I just cried and cried. I had been traveling through so much terror; I had begun to doubt that I would ever see him again. And now, here he was. It seemed like such a long wait.

Immediately we started the process of getting a Visa for me to travel to the United States. Since I was classified as a refuge, we went to the United Nations office. I recall thinking how odd it was that weeks before I had been traveling by foot or by camel in the dead of night, and now I was riding in Judy's car, being chauffeured by her driver, sleeping in a cool, clean bed, eating good food in a beautiful mansion, a total opposite of before. ALL GLORY TO GOD!

The Lord is my strength and my shield;
My heart trusts in Him, and I am helped;
Therefore, my heart triumphs, And with my
song I shall thank Him. (Psalm 28:7 NASB)

At the United Nations office my fiancé and I explained that I was carrying a refugee passport. The UN official was not kind. In fact, he was upset.

"How do you know this man?" he demanded, wanting to know about our relationship. "He's white, you are black. He's American, you are a refugee. How do you know him?" Americans do not have a good name in Egypt despite the fact they are the most benevolent people in the world giving to all who need.

Rather than answer such inappropriate questioning, we decided to leave the United Nations office. I told my fiancé "We need to leave this office right now!" We went back to Judy's house and told Judy and Dr. Watson what had happened.

"AB," Dr. Watson said sternly. "This is not right. I'm going to talk to the American Embassy."

Dr. Watson became my advocate at the American Embassy. He went and told them the whole story of how he knew me, and how I had worked for the Americans before they were forced out of Ethiopia. Dr. Watson insisted that I was a very respectable woman with high integrity. He assured them that my character was above reproach and that as a mother of three I was not a threat to the US.

She's a person of high character and the mother of three," Dr. Watson told them. "AB has worked hard for the American attaché in Ethiopia. She deserves our thanks and respect."

The American Embassy officer said, "We can take care of this." He sealed my visa and we were approved.

PART 3

Growing Up in Ethiopia

I was born in Addis Ababa, Ethiopia, the oldest child within the marriage between my father and my mother. My father had a son out of wedlock, born during World War II, before he and my mother were married. A couple years after I was born my mother gave birth to my little brother. When he was less than forty days old my mother tired of the responsibilities of parenting and left our family.

My father was a physician for the Ethiopian prison and he also ran a medical clinic at home. Like many other families we owned and operated a small farm right in the city of Addis Ababa with a creamery. Our family was upper middle class with a few servants to help run the various facets of our lives. A servant took over, looking after my brother and me as my father went through a series of wives looking for a proper mother to care for us.

My first stepmother was a good cook and kept my brother and I clean and well cared for. She and my father had a daughter, and I was delighted to have a baby sister. But this stepmother wouldn't allow my brother or me to play. She would dress us up and expect us to sit on the bench in front of our house and watch the neighborhood children run and play. If we forgot to sit still, as preschool children often do, she would get really upset. She had an uncontrollable temper. My father was fearful of her temper and thought she might actually harm my brother or me, and before long my father divorced her. She took my baby sister and left us motherless once more.

My father was my joy. He loved me and my brother so much and doted on us whenever he was home. More than anything my father wanted my brother and me to have a good mother. Out of desperation to provide that, he married again to a woman who had two school age girls. These girls were extremely mean to me and took over our home acting like the queens of the house. Even worse, they were physically abusive to me often hitting me and punishing me with painful consequences. But what was more disconcerting to my father was my new stepmother's inability to cook a proper meal. When my father's traditional Easter gift of fresh yogurt and homemade bread was spoiled with her rock-hard bread, he let her go and I was once again without a mother.

Thinking back on the succession of women that my father married, trying to find a satisfactory mother for my brother and me, I know that my father could have been more careful. There were dozens of community members who would have looked after his children. He did not need to marry so quickly. But I think that my father's desperation was bigger than his need.

My biological mother came to visit occasionally. She would arrive with a sweater, a dress or perfume for me, and I never quite knew what to do with her gifts. I was excited to see her when she came, but I wasn't sad when she left. Even as a young child, I knew that my mother wasn't really interested in the responsibility or commitment of being a parent.

Growing up female in Ethiopia was different than in the United States. Women were second class citizens with few legal rights. Laws did not protect women or children. But my father didn't seem to mind that I was a girl. I was the apple of his eye.

I loved working with my father in his medical clinic. I remember when an epidemic took over our community and many people were coming to see my father with severe rashes and fevers. I was seven years old when my father gave me gloves and taught me how to scrub the wounds and scraping them with a scalpel. He valued me as a person, and never discounted me because I was female. He taught me how to make decisions, how to think through problems, and to act with confidence.

Even as a child I had responsibilities. Besides helping in my father's medical practice, I helped care for the animals on our farm. I remember being about six years old when the shepherd boy who looked after our cows in the pasture was ignoring a bloated calf.

"Aren't you going to do something?" I asked this shepherd boy who was about 10 or 11 years old. The calf was lying flat, breathing hard, with a huge, bloated stomach.

"What would I do?" the boy asked. "The calf is sick. I can't fix him."

I ran down the hill as fast as my little legs could carry me. I had seen my father treat bloated animals before and I wanted to help this calf. I went into my father's clinic, grabbed a knife and ran back up the hill.

Gasping for breath when I reached the calf, I surveyed the situation. I had seen my father puncture a bloated animal's belly before. I didn't know for sure where to cut, but I felt confident in my six-year-old wisdom that doing something to help was better than doing nothing. I wanted to make sure that this valuable animal did not die, but I wasn't really sure where to poke the knife.

Closing my eyes tight I raised my arm over my head and brought the knife down, stabbing the calf in the stomach. A whoosh of putrid, stinky air came blowing out. Oh my! Did it ever stink! But, in a few minutes, the calf was standing up and eating! My father was so proud of my quick thinking and how the calf was saved.

It wasn't the first time I embarrassed the shepherd boy. Once I complained to him that he was using a dirty bucket to collect the milk and made him wash the bucket—twice. The shepherd boy got so mad at me one day that he chased me down the hill with a shovel!

I had the usual bumps and bruises all children have growing up. But I remember a time when I thought for sure that I was going to die. I was just a little girl and I was with my friends celebrating an Ethiopian holiday sort of like the American Halloween. Our holiday was only celebrated by girls and we sang a song about our national flower around our neighborhood. It was during this celebration that my friends and I decided we were old enough to venture out of our neighborhood.

To get to our destination we had to walk over a dangerous water walkway which was located with a steep hill on one side and a ditch with swift running water on the other. In my bravery I slipped and fell landing precariously with my feet hanging over the bank of the river and my chest on a rock. It was too slippery for my friends to safely reach me and they were too small to pull me up. I lay there stunned and I could hear the girls crying and wailing in fear. Then suddenly a man we had never seen in our neighborhood before appeared. He reached out and pulled me up the side of the slippery bank to safety.

"You saved me." I looked around for my friends who were running for help.

"Let's see, are you hurt?" He helped me up off the ground and turned me around. "Nope, you look just fine." Then the stranger gently swatted my behind, "Now stay away from the water," he said sternly. I started to walk toward my friends and turned remembering then to thank the stranger. He was gone. I believe God was watching out for me that day.

For He will give His angels orders concerning you, To protect you in all your ways. On their hands they will lift you up, So that

you do not strike your foot against a stone.
(Psalm 91:11-12 NASB)

I have great memories of going to my grandfather's house. He ran a carriage rental company with 12 carriages. When I visited him, I was the only girl who helped at his business. Grandfather would allow me to tag long as he took care of business. At the end of the day, my grandfather put me in charge of collecting the fare money from the carriage drivers.

I was a small girl about eight years old living in a male dominated culture, yet I would stand at the door as the men came in from their shifts. "Is this all you made today?" I would ask. "Come on, pay up!" I would insist that they pay my grandfather what they owed him.

My grandfather didn't pay me to work for him, but he taught me valuable lessons about owning a business and making a profit. He taught me the value of running an honest business. My uncles stole money from my grandfather, but I took Grandfather's money and hid it in the grain. The men chased me and threatened me, but I slipped through their hands and kept safe.

My father doted on my brother and me and always employed loyal servants to take care of us while he was away at work. But eventually he decided to try again to find a proper mother for us. He went back to his homeland, Asmara in Eritrea, to find a wife. He said he needed to be blessed by the elders and fathers at his church so he could find a wife. He thought if he found a nice woman who could be blessed by the family, she would be more successful as a mother for my brother and me.

Unfortunately, the woman my father found in Asmara turned out to be the meanest of the mean women in my life. She was a faithful wife to my father, but she was extremely unkind and cruel to me. I did my best to stay out of her way. Each day I would wait for my father to come home and I lived for the quiet moments of encouragement that he would share with me.

My father had big plans for me and together we talked about them often. His dream was for me to go to medical school and to become a doctor. He encouraged me in my studies and had faith in my ability to pursue a medical career. He included me in his practice whenever he could. I helped in the clinic at home and on weekends I went with him to bring food to the prison.

I always felt loved when my father and I shared an activity. I loved my father dearly, but so did our entire community. My father practiced traditional medicine, but he also practiced homeopathic medicine. One of the mysteries my father seemed to be able to heal was infertility. Women would come to my father unable to conceive and with his homeopathic treatment many of them were with child in a few months. As result, my father had 84 godchildren in our city!

The people in the community came to our clinic and watched as my father would heal the ill in various ways. Often patients were unable to pay for his services, but my father always told them, "That's okay, you can pay next time." There were many, many "next times" in my father's bookkeeping.

I remember that I was barely twelve when I started my first menstrual period. No one had ever told me about how a young girl's body matures into womanhood, and I didn't know what was wrong with me. I couldn't imagine talking to my stepmother about it, and even my father's guidance wasn't in my realm of possibilities for something so private.

So, I just went to school, and I didn't even tell my best girlfriend, Elana. All day at school I was very quiet and uncomfortable, and no one knew my secret. After school I went to Elena's house for a snack. Elana was being raised by her very well-to-do grandmother, who was a close friend of my father's.

"I saw a girl today who had a spot on her dress," I lied as Elana and I nibbled on cookies. Before I could elaborate on my lie, Elana's grandmother spoke up.

"Oh, poor little girl," Elana's grandma said sympathetically. "She wasn't prepared."

"What do you mean?" I asked.

"You and Elana are both going to start your periods very soon," she explained. "You will need to be prepared so you don't stain your clothing."

"What do you mean?" I asked curiously. "Periods only happen to women who are married. We aren't married!"

Elana's grandmother smiled, "No, child. You don't have to be married to begin having periods," and she went on to explain all about it.

I started crying and I confessed to Elana's grandma that I had lied, and that it was me who had the spot on my dress. I asked her dozens of questions and patiently she answered every one of them. Then she took Elana and me shopping and bought everything we needed for menstruation days.

But that wasn't the end of it. That week Elana's grandmother met with my father, and she was really upset with him, a physician, who had neglected to teach his daughter about something so important. I couldn't talk to my father or stepmother about it because I was too embarrassed, but I loved Elana's grandmother for teaching me something that girls should learn from their mothers.

As I listened to Elana's grandmother assure me that having periods wasn't anything to be ashamed of, I believe at that moment it opened the door of hatred toward my biological mother. I started having anger against my birth mother. I began to realize that if my mother had been here, and if she hadn't left us, I would have known all the things that Elana's grandmother had to teach me. As that door opened, it was as if I gave myself permission to be angry with my mother for the neglect and abandonment that had been festering for 10 years and all at once I didn't care if my mother ever visited me again.

By the time I was twelve years old my third stepmother and my father had three children together. My stepmother was pregnant with a fourth child, when one night, my wonderful, healthy and hearty father died suddenly in his sleep.

I was devastated and my whole world tipped upside down. My own mother had left me long ago and this stepmother was so mean I did not want to live with her. Through the shock and grief of losing my beloved father, my mind whirled around the big question, what was I going to do?

My father's funeral was postponed while we waited for people to arrive from around the region. All the tribes were coming to mourn my father's death. Some came to sing, some to dance, and some to pound their chests. My father was honored and revered by thousands of people and the funeral procession was long and drawn out as everyone came to pay their respects. Some of the mourners were on horseback with horses decorated in bright costumes, some walked and all were deeply saddened that my father had died at the young age of fifty-five.

> *So you have sorrow now, but I will see you again; then you will rejoice, and no one can rob you of that joy. (John 16:22 NLT)*

My world was in chaos. I didn't know what would happen to me. I knew I didn't want to live with my stepmother, but where did I want to live? I surely didn't want to live with my biological mother. Questions swirled in my head. Where would I sleep? Where would I go to school? How could I become a doctor? Who would take care of me? What would become of my father's practice? Where would I get food?

Do not be anxious about anything, but in everything by prayer and pleading with thanksgiving let your requests be made known to God. (Philippians 4:6 NASB)

My uncle came from Eritrea for the funeral. As people began to discuss what would happen to all of my father's children, my uncle spoke up. "AB's father wanted her to go to school and become a doctor. I'm going to take her, and she will follow that path."

My birth mother was there, and she spoke up, "No, I'll take care of her. You have no right to interfere."

My uncle argued and pressed on that I was to return to Eritrea where I could study to become a physician and marry into the family tribe.

But my mother continued to argue, "No! I am her mother! She will go with me!" and my fate was sealed.

My mother packed me up and she rented a house in a neighborhood of several single men. Then with no explanation of where she was going or when she'd be back, she left town. I was mourning my father so deeply and terrified of living alone in a neighborhood filled with a bunch of single men. At night I would lock up the doors and pile pots and pans in front of each of them to serve as an alarm if someone tried to get in.

One day, after a few weeks of living on my own, my mother returned with an arranged marriage planned.

"AB, you're going to marry a truck driver," she said firmly. "He's a good man. He will make a fine husband for you."

"I'm barely thirteen!" I cried. "I don't want to marry a truck driver or anyone else." This man was in his thirties and I was not at all interested in becoming his bride.

"You will listen to me and marry him," she insisted.

I went to my friends at school and told them about my mother's plans. My friends started making fun of me and I realized that my feelings weren't wrong. I decided that I was not going to marry this truck driver or anyone else my mother brought home.

Mother was furious with me, stomped out and left me alone in that house again.

When she left this time, I ached inside with the grief of missing my father, and the anguish of having a mother with so little regard for me. I was still terrified that one of the men in the neighborhood would try to come into my room at night, and I piled chairs and other furniture against the doors as I set my pots and pans alarm. And that night, I had a terrible nightmare.

To this day I vividly recall that terrible dream. I was walking along a country road when several men dressed in white Arabian robes began following me. All I could see was their pitch-black faces looming within their white robes and turbans. They were behind me and I began walking faster to get away.

Then I looked up ahead and there was another group of men who looked exactly like the others, coming from the way I was headed. I turned left and began running up a hill as fast as I could go trying to escape. On one side of the hill was a deep ditch and on the other a steep rocky wall. I looked back and the men were coming behind me.

Then in my dream a bicycle suddenly appeared. I jumped on the bicycle and began pedaling as fast as I could. The road was steep, but I pushed hard on the pedals and began to climb up the road. I was getting away, but the men were still chasing me, chanting "Ho-o, ho-o, ho-o," in a loud, creepy chant.

Then my dream became even more terrifying. As I frantically rode the bicycle up the hill, I looked up and saw that the road was suddenly filled with more men coming down the hill dressed the same, and chanting the same evil sound.

In my dream, I was being pursued from behind me and in front of me. I had nowhere to turn to escape. I jumped off the bicycle and began to scream loud, hysterical screams, and I woke up. Later I heard someone trying to break into my room. I was filled with paralyzing fear as I sorted out the terror of my dream and the very real threat of someone trying to get into my room.

This horrifying dream pushed me into telling my best friend, Siga Laken, about being abandoned by my mother. When I told her that my mother had left me again, Siga said, "I'm telling my mom. You're moving in with us."

And just like that, I moved in with Siga's family. They were a wealthy family and paid for all of my expenses. I took a few items from the house where my mother had left me, but basically, I arrived with nothing. Siga's family didn't mind and soon I had what I needed.

Siga's mother was more of a mother to me than anyone had ever been in my life and soon she was more than a foster care giver to me; she became my godmother. Siga's mother assumed the role of a mother which I dearly wanted. It is the custom in Ethiopia that if someone desires to become a godmother, an official ceremony must be held through the church with witnesses to the event. Siga's family spoke to the priest and a big celebration and feast was held as she became my godmother.

Siga's parents bought me a new dress and made sure that my hair was especially styled for the great celebration. At the party a bowl of pure honey was prepared. After a prayer, Siga's mother dipped her thumb into the honey and I sucked it off. She did this three times, and I sucked the honey from her thumb three times. And then, Siga's mother was my official godmother. God provided all of this as part of his promise to be the Father to the fatherless.

A father of the fatherless and a judge for the widows, Is God in His holy dwelling. (Psalm 68:5 NASB)

With my mother out of the picture and Siga's mother my official godmother, I finally felt safe. Surrounded by people who cared about me and provided a home for me should have been a place to thrive. But as I matured into a young woman, my grief magnified, and I felt deep pain and sorrow as I mourned my father. And in my fifteen-year-old teenage wisdom, I decided that I could fill this void in my life if I got married.

Marriage and Turmoil

I met a handsome Ethiopian man name Gebermedhin. He was in his thirties and worked as an accountant. Gebermedhin offered me what I wanted most in the world—my own home. Despite my godmother's disapproval, I ran away and married Gebermedhin when I was fifteen.

> *Through overconfidence comes nothing but strife, But wisdom is with those who receive counsel. (Proverbs 13:10 NASB)*

At first, it was wonderful. I had servants to help me run our home and I enjoyed keeping house and looking after Gebermedhin. But before long I discovered that Gebermedhin was addicted to alcohol and most of his fine salary went to pay for his drinking. Gebermedhin came home late every night, drunk and mean-spirited. Soon he began to beat me in his alcoholic rage. I was distraught because I couldn't conceive a child, and I justified Gebermedhin's violent behavior with my inability to give him an heir.

Despite Gebermedhin's abuse, I chose to stay with him. I grew up without a mother and now my father was gone. It was clear that Gebermedhin was nothing like my kind, loving father, but still, I wanted to stay with him. After three years, I finally conceived a child and our beautiful daughter, Sara, was born. I thought perhaps things would be all right, since Gebermedhin had the presence of mind not to beat me when I was pregnant. Soon after Sara's birth his wrath returned, and I was tormented once more with Gebermedhin's beating. But, just a few months after Sara's birth, I again conceived and the beatings stopped as Gebermedhin awaited the birth of our second child, one he hoped would be a boy this time.

Throughout my marriage to Gebermedhin, my father's dreams of me becoming a doctor were always in my head. I didn't want to become a doctor, but I did want a formal education. So I enrolled in some college classes wanting to finish an accounting degree. With a baby at home and being pregnant it wasn't easy, but I was dedicated to working on my education whenever I could find a moment for myself. My husband was not at all supportive of my education.

"You can't go to school!" Gebermedhin shouted at me one day when I was working on my homework.

"Why not?" I asked.

"Because I said so!" was his angry reply. I knew he was thinking that my college classes were costing money that he wouldn't be able to spend on booze.

"I will be able to get a good job," I told him. "Our lives will be better if we have two incomes."

"You do not need to go to college!" Gebermedhin yelled at me.

I had an accounting homework spreadsheet on the counter. Gebermedhin tore it up and stormed out of the house. I remained calm. I studied with a group of people, and they helped me redo my homework before the class.

A few weeks later Gebermedhin applied for a new job and forged a signature on a recommendation. He wasn't arrested, but he was fired from his accounting job and not hired for the new one. Gebermedhin said he was trying to find a new job, but he wasn't able to secure employment.

I decided that I would start a business to support us. Even though my time was consumed with Sara and my college classes, I decided to start a bakery business. Engera is an Ethiopian flat bread that looks like a sponge. Near my home was a large upscale apartment building. The people who lived there could not bake in their apartments, so I went door to door in that apartment building and offered to bake Engera for them and deliver it to their doors. That first day I had forty-three clients!

May the kindness of the Lord our God be upon us; And confirm for us the work of our hands; Yes, confirm the work of our hands. (Psalm 90:17 NASB)

I hadn't even started anything other than lining up people to buy my bread. I didn't have any money to buy grain, I had no idea how much each loaf of bread would cost me compared to what I had quoted as a price to my clients. I had no business plan.

My girlfriend's father was impressed with my entrepreneurship, and he bought the grain. And so, I began my bread baking business. I found two women to help me, and I went back out knocking on doors and found even more clients. Suddenly I was making a lot of money with my bread business. I was very excited that I could provide food for my children.

When you eat the fruit of the labor of your hands, You will be happy and it will go well for you. (Psalm 128:2 NASB)

Gebermedhin was happy for a while, because now he had plenty of money to drink. But before long he was back to his same old mean tactics. I had signed several more clients to buy bread and was excited about the income I was providing while completing my degree. Gebermedhin came home and again was verbally abusive insisting that I didn't need to go to college. In his fury he poured coffee all over the homework I had just finished. He insisted that he didn't want me to go to college; he wanted me to stay at home and have another baby.

And then, as quickly as my bread baking business grew, it ceased. A member of the royal family opened an

Ethiopian delicatessen in the bottom floor of the apartment building where most of my clients lived. The deli offered bread, coffee, honey, wine, spices and all the things traditional to Ethiopian cuisine. My bread customers were not welcome at the deli unless they bought their bread from the deli and soon, they all left me and began to buy their bread there.

> *He said, "Naked I came from my mother's womb, And naked I shall return there. The Lord gave and the Lord has taken away. Blessed be the name of the Lord. (Job 1:21 NASB)*

My college classes were held in the evening and Gebermedhin refused to give me a ride to school. My friend, Aberashe, was taking the same course, so I just called her and she drove me. But Gebermedhin was putting up other roadblocks toward my education. Even though I was the one who had been making the money at our house, Gebermedhin refused to give me the money to pay for my classes. I didn't know what to do about my tuition.

I went to the financial aid office and explained my dilemma. They graciously allowed me to continue my classes and finish my degree. But the school would not allow me to walk in the line of the graduation ceremony or give me my diploma until I paid the $2000 that I still owed.

I took a job as a receptionist with John Deere Tractor Company in the mechanics department. I was so happy that I would have enough money to pay my final tuition payment to finish my college degree. I began to squirrel money away to pay the final tuition due at the college. Once again God was giving me favor as my funds built quickly toward my degree. I didn't have it paid in time to walk in the graduation ceremony, but I was able to pay what I owed and obtain my diploma within a few months.

I can do all things through Him who strengthens me. (Philippians 4:13 NASB)

My second child, Elizabeth, arrived 15 months after Sara's birth. My two little girls were beautiful and I devoted myself to them and to keeping our home. But even with our two perfect girls, our home clean and meals prepared, Gebermedhin continued to beat me. Soon more of his salary was going to pay his debts at the bars than what he was bringing home. I didn't know anything about the disease of alcoholism; I just knew that when Gebermedhin came home, I was going to be beaten.

I recall one day when Gebermedhin came home, drunk, angry and spoiling for a fight. He began his usual verbal abuse and when he came after me to hit me, I ran out the door. I just kept running down the street thinking that if I waited awhile, he'd calm down, go to bed and then I would go back home. I looked over my shoulder and Gebermedhin was coming after me. He was much bigger and stronger than I, and even in his drunken state he was gaining on me. He was yelling at me and calling me names threatening to hurt me.

There was a wedding in our neighborhood and the neighbors were singing a song outside. I knew that I couldn't outrun Gebermedhin, so I just blended into the crowd singing. Gebermedhin lost me but began wandering through the wedding guests. The neighbors grabbed me and pushed me into the kitchen. They hid me there all afternoon giving me food and respite. Later I went home, after Gebermedhin left the house. Deep inside I knew that I didn't want to live like this.

We argued constantly bringing in family from both sides to counsel with us, yet Gebermedhin insisted that he didn't want a divorce. He claimed that he wanted his family together and that he wanted more children. He promised to change, but he didn't. I was so young and naïve, I thought maybe he's right. Maybe he just needs more children to come home to at the end of a day. When I discovered that I was pregnant again I thought Gebermedhin would be thrilled. I asked him to take me to the doctor for my first check up and he said, "I'll take you to the doctor and then give you a knife and you can take the child out."

I was shocked and horrified. Abortion was not a consideration for me. I loved this unborn child and I could hardly believe that Gebermedhin was being so cruel. I began to make plans to leave him.

Holy Pork! I'm Not a Sinner

When I was a child, I knew that my father was a Christian. But my dad didn't like the church. He found all the rules, politics and gossip within the church tiresome so he did not take me or my siblings to church. But in his clinic Dad had a place to pray. I remember going to this special place in the clinic and just sitting there and feeling some kind of peace in this place. My dad always told he wanted me to choose my own religion.

My faith began to grow early in my life for in Ethiopia before you go to regular school you have to read the Old Testament of the Bible three times; the Old Testament. The Priest is the one who teaches children during this time and I recall it being the most boring thing in the world. Each day I was forced to just sit and read that huge book written mostly in Elizabethan language. There are all those strange names, 'begets', prophesies, and it can take a child up to two years to complete. I was disciplined to complete this task and knew I would get a spanking if I didn't sit still and concentrate.

I remember visiting with the local missionaries and attending the mission gatherings learning more about

God from them. I studied the Ten Commandments and Psalms. I remember thinking how clever we children were when the missionaries asked us to sing. We would all sing an off- color, inappropriate song in our native language. It was a horrible song, but the missionaries didn't know that and they laughed and clapped and asked us to sing it again. Rebellion was buried in my heart, but God was in my shadow following me each day.

> *Do not be deceived, God is not mocked; for whatever a person sows, this he will also reap. (Galatians 6:7 NASB)*

Abebech, my godmother, was a practicing Christian insisted Siga and I go to the Ethiopian Orthodox church all the time. Siga and I used to sneak out on Saturday nights and have a hard time waking up on Sunday mornings. Abebech had no sympathy for us and would pour cold water on us to get us up on Sunday mornings.

The church services were long and boring. There were no chairs so we had to stand for over an hour of the traditional service. Most of the preaching was in Hebrew and Siga and I couldn't understand it. But each Sunday Abebech dragged us to church. Sadly, I had no idea what I was doing there other than pleasing Abebech.

When the girls were little, I bought Mortadella, which is Italian processed pork. I thought it would make good sandwiches for the children. I brought it home and placed it in the refrigerator knowing that the servants would find it for lunch the next day.

I had no idea what an uproar bringing home Mortadella would cause. My servants were terribly upset and insisted that the house was unholy because the processed pork was in our refrigerator. They had called the Priest and my biological mother even showed up, insisting that there were dire consequences for having this unholy meat in our house.

Acts NASB 11:9 But a voice from heaven answered a second time,

'What God has cleansed, no longer consider unholy.'

Father John shook his head and said, "AB, you must be re-baptized."

I was outraged. "No! Show me in the Bible where it says that a person has to be re-baptized if she brings Mortadella into her house!" I demanded.

The priest couldn't show me any information about it in the Bible but insisted that it must be done.

"No!" I refused.

"Then you are forbidden to come to the church," Father John said, sternly.

After that I started taking my children to the Southern Baptist church down the street. The music was loud and lively, and I could understand the preaching. The children and I liked Pastor Wood and his wife, Mrs. Wood, and enjoyed talking with them after services. Then one day, all of a sudden, Pastor and Miss Wood started coming to visit me. They wanted to talk to me about becoming "born again."

I liked learning about the Bible and how God cared for me. I liked knowing that God loved me, but Pastor and Mrs. Wood said that I was a sinner.

"What do you mean, I'm a sinner?" I asked, hurt and a bit shocked. "I'm not a sinner." I defended myself. "Sure, I stole sugar and raisins when I was a little girl, but I didn't kill anybody. I'm not a sinner."

But Pastor and Mrs. Wood wouldn't let me go. They just came back again and again, each time with another message of God's love and asking if I was ready to ask God to forgive me and welcome Jesus into my heart.

As much as I liked Pastor and Mrs. Wood, I thought they would take away my short Tina Turner style skirts. I liked dressing like a "hot mama," and I thought they would take away my makeup and my high heel shoes. But they didn't. Instead, they just continued to encourage me to admit my sins and to ask Jesus to be my Savior.

One day I decided that I'd had just about enough of this sinner nonsense so just to get rid of them, I agreed to ask God to forgive me for my sins (which I didn't really have) and to accept Jesus Christ as my Savior.

Pastor led me in the Christian Sinner's Prayer. "God, I know that I am a sinner. I know that I deserve the consequences of my sin. However, I am trusting in Jesus Christ as my Savior. I believe that His death and resurrection provided for my forgiveness. I trust in Jesus and Jesus alone as my personal Lord and Savior. Thank you, Lord, for saving me and forgiving me!"

If you confess with your mouth Jesus as Lord, and believe in your heart that God raised Him from the dead, you will be saved; for with the heart a person believes, resulting in righteousness, and with the mouth he confesses, resulting in salvation. (Romans 10:9-10 NASB)

Even with my rebellious heart, something happened inside of me when I prayed that prayer. I can't explain it. I didn't want to believe it. Yet, there was definitely a change in my soul. Suddenly I had hope that there was something out there in the universe to help me raise my kids by myself.

When I accepted Jesus as my Savior there was a powerful, magnificent, colorful light that filled me. It was a jumble of shades and sensations that went through my body and it felt so good. I didn't know what it was and it scared me a bit, but it was so beautiful that my only reaction was that I wanted to feel that way again and again. It changed me in ways I didn't expect; my atmosphere, my persona, and my countenance. I had fear, but I had divine courage. I had sadness, but I was also comforted. It was hard for me to even tell people what I was feeling because I likened it to being part of a stained-glass window with bright colors and light swirling within and around me.

And there is salvation in no one else; for there is no other name under heaven that has been given among mankind by which we must be saved. (Acts 4:12 NASB)

I started saying things to myself. "My kids will be happy. My kids will be free. I will be free. I won't be afraid anymore."

I started feeling lighthearted and distinctly less tense. Things didn't bother me anymore. In the past I was usually happy and joyful, but now I had a different kind of joy and happiness. I still had fear, but now I had a divine courage and it felt good. I was 23 years old and I had just been born again.

I decided that I would have to wait for the birth of my third baby before I could leave the violence of being Gebermedhin's wife. At least Gebermedhin wouldn't hit me now that I was pregnant.

My degree was in accounting, so I continued to look for a job where I could use my knowledge and make a little more money. Soon I found one with Pepsi Cola in the accounting department, working for the chief accountant.

It was difficult working full time, being pregnant and having two toddlers at home. The servants looked after the girls while I was at work and helped keep up the home. And since I had decided that I was leaving Gebermedhin as soon as the baby was born, I was determined to stick with the job and the exhausting schedule.

Just when I had learned the routine at Pepsi, the company went through a down-sizing and laid many people off. I was one of them.

Do not be anxious about anything, but in everything by prayer and pleading with thanksgiving let your requests be made known to God. And the peace of God, which surpasses all comprehension, will guard your hearts and minds in Christ Jesus. (Philippians 4:6-7 NASB)

Undaunted, I still planned my escape from Gebermedhin. My plan was well thought out. I wanted to have the baby while I was still living with Gebermedhin because I was afraid that Gebermedhin would claim the baby wasn't his if I left him before the birth. With no job and three children to support it was going to be more difficult to leave than I had hoped, but I was determined to escape the violent environment. My son, Yohannes was born, and in the Ethiopian culture, having a son was a fine achievement for Gebermedhin. Yet he was not happy.

I cleaned and organized the house and then packed the children's things. Then I sat down with my two servants and over coffee I explained that I was leaving.

"I'm sorry," I told them. "I cannot pay you. You will have to find a new job."

My two servants looked at each other and then at me. "No!" they both cried. "We are going wherever you go!"

"But I can't pay you!" I cried. "I don't even know how I will feed the children." There was no child support or alimony in Ethiopia. I was going off on my own and would be the sole support of my household.

"We will eat, when you eat," my servant said. "We will sleep where you sleep."

Ruth 1:16-17 NASB 16 But Ruth said, "Do not plead with me to leave you or to turn back from following you; for where you go, I will go, and where you sleep,

I will sleep. Your people shall be my people, and your God, my God.

17 Where you die, I will die, and there I will be buried. May the Lord do so to me, and worse, if anything but death separates me from you."

And with that my servants each grabbed the bags I packed; I took the children and we left. I rented a one room house in a gated neighborhood for a very low price. It wasn't fancy, but I felt safe from Gebermedhin there. I didn't know how I would feed the children, but I had faith in God that he would see me through. I wasn't afraid; I knew I was doing the right thing.

That first day, my neighbor gave me $20. I gave it to one of the servants and she went to the market and brought back all sorts of good things to eat. That first night we had spaghetti and we all slept on the floor, except for Yohannes, who slept in a baby bed.

The next day I called all my friends.

"I need your help," I said. "Please don't ask questions, just come to this address. Bring a lunch for you and one for me. Please don't go to Gebermedhin's house. I don't live there anymore and I'm not going back."

All of the people I called showed up. They each brought two lunches and I was able to feed all the children and servants. They gave me about $175 and wished me well. Each of them went back to work. By evening I had a bed, a refrigerator, oil, groceries and I felt so blessed. We slept on the floor, and when I closed my eyes that night, I felt safe and so happy. I knew that God would see me through this crisis.

Within a few days, I found a job at the US Air Force base as a part time Operator/Receptionist and within a week or so I secured a second part-time job at the American Country Club doing their bookkeeping. When there was an opening at the movie theatre to work weekends, I snapped that up as well, and with all that hard work, I was getting rich. The cost of living in Ethiopia was very low and by working so many hours, with so little living expenses, I was able to provide for myself, three children and two servants in that little house.

And God is able to make all grace overflow to you, so that, always having all sufficiency in everything, you may have an abundance for every good deed. (2 Corinthians 9:8 NASB)

The civil unrest in Ethiopia continued with the new King's regime. Children were being killed in the new Communist regime, for they were the best educated in the country. Children between nine and fourteen were herded into groups and slaughtered. The woman who lived in the house next door to me lost three of her children to this genocide. Her school-age children were kidnapped and taken to a warehouse where they were murdered.

While I was safer in this little house without an abusive husband, each day brought my children closer to an age where they would be targets.

Kidnapped

My servants remained faithful. It was a tight fit in our little house, but we were happy, and the children were thriving; until Gebermedhin decided to come after me.

When I refused to discuss returning home with Gebermedhin he was furious. "You'll be sorry!" he screamed at me.

I was worried at the threat. Gebermedhin had been increasingly cruel to me. There was no telling what he might do to me or the children.

Yohannes was the happiest, chubbiest, most robust little baby in all of Ethiopia. His big dark eyes sparkled when he laughed and his chubby arms and legs were always wiggling. His laughter filled our little house and his sisters and my servants adored him. He was a hearty eater and I loved to snuggle with my perfect little child.

One day, when Yohannes was about six months old, I came home from work to find my servants crying and terribly upset.

"Gebermedhin kidnapped Yohannes," my servant said. "He just came in and took him. We couldn't stop him."

My heart stopped in terror. I was so scared. I didn't know what Gebermedhin might do to Yohannes. I went to my ex-husband's house determined to get Johanas's back.

"Where is my son?" I demanded. I ran from room to room, looking for my baby. But the child wasn't anywhere in Gebermedhin's house. "Where did you take him?" I pleaded, hysterical with fear.

"What? You lost my child?" Gebermedhin roared at me. "He's not here. What did you do with him?" Gebermedhin tried to hit me again and I ran out of the house and down the street terrified of what this crazy man might have done with my son.

I came home, sobbing uncontrollably. I begged God to keep my baby safe and to return him to me. My friends were sending up prayers from all over. My friend Aberashe went to fasting and to the Gedam prayer place. In my hysteria I went to the police.

> *For I am the Lord your God who takes hold*
> *of your right hand, Who says to you, "Do not*
> *fear, I will help you." (Isaiah 41:13 NASB)*

I was so upset and frantic that no one at the Police Station would even listen to me. They just thought I was crazy and sent me away. There was no one to help me find my baby.

With my three jobs there had been little time for anything else, but now I stopped working at all three places and focused on finding Yohannes. After I calmed down,

I decided to go to the Chief of Police to talk to him. But I knew that after my first attempt at getting the police to help me, I would have to catch the Police Chief outside of the office, maybe in the parking lot when he arrived for work. I studied where he parked, what time it was, and how he entered the building every day.

Gathering my courage, I waited for him to arrive one morning. I stopped him in the parking lot.

"Mr. Officer," I cried. "My baby boy has been kidnapped by his father. But he doesn't have him."

"Well, report it," he snapped, not stopping to look at me.

"Please, sir!" I was crying. "I did report it. But no one would help me."

"Go on, woman," the police chief said, turning to look at me. "If the baby is with his father, that's how it should be." He turned back to walk away.

I reached for his hand. "Please," I begged through my tears, "He doesn't have him. My baby's father has hidden the boy away and I'm afraid for my child's life. Please, please, I need your help."

The police chief shook my hand away. "Get away from me!" he said sternly, and began walking toward the building.

I was devastated and furious. I gathered my composure and just as he reached the door to the building I shouted, "Commander. What would you do if one of your children was kidnapped? Would you come to work? Would you just go on and live your life?"

He turned to look at me.

I continued shouting, "If your son was missing, what you would do? Would you expect someone in authority to help you find him?" the tears were pouring down my face. "Please, why won't you help me?"

The police chief looked at the man at the door. He nodded toward me. "Bring her in," he said, and then he walked into the building. I was escorted to the police chief's office.

"All right," he said from across his desk. "Tell me the story."

I started to tell how Gebermedhin had come to my house and taken Yohannes when the chief interrupted me, "How do you know your ex-husband took him?" he asked.

"My servants saw him!" I cried.

"But if he is the boy's father, you don't have a case," the police chief said.

"Why don't you give me a chance?" I begged. "Give me a policeman and I'll show you where Gebermedhin is. Please bring him here for questioning. Ask him what he has done with my son."

Asking to have Gebermedhin brought into the police station was not a smart thing for me to do. If Gebermedhin was found innocent, I knew that the police would put me in jail. But I was desperate to find my baby. I looked at the Police Chief's big office. The floor was cement. I threw myself down on the floor and rolled back and forth, back and forth in a log roll, in my grief for my son.

"Get up! Get up!" the police chief yelled at me. "Okay, okay, you win. I'll give you two policemen and the car with the machine gun. Take them to Gebermedhin. But if Gebermedhin is innocent of what you say, you will be in jail."

I got to my feet, wiping my eyes, sniffling, and gaining a spark of hope that I might at last receive the help I needed to find my son.

I sighed. "Okay. Let's go."

The police officer drove me and another officer to Gebermedhin's house where we found him in bed, drunk, as usual. The police officers rousted him out of bed and began to ask where Johanas was.

"She lost my son," Gebermedhin said defiantly. "She lost him and now she's blaming me."

I was frantic, wanting Gebermedhin to just tell me where Yohannes was. I threw myself down on the floor again and I rolled on the floor back and forth, back and forth like a log on the floor. I don't know why I did this; it's not a common practice in Ethiopia. I was so distraught with anguish I just fell, and I thought I would be able to gain sympathy from the police with this desperate display of grief.

"See, she's crazy," Gebermedhin told the police. In Ethiopian culture, women are second class citizens and have very few rights. I expected the police to take Gebermedhin's side.

The police officer helped me up, "Come on, get up lady," he said as he pulled me to my feet. I looked at

Gebermedhin and begged him to tell me where Yohannes was.

One of the officers said, "Okay, we're going to figure this out in jail," and pulled his handcuffs out.

Gebermedhin blew out a big sigh and frowned. "Okay, okay," he said, rubbing his dark hair and stubbled face with his hand, "I'll tell you where he is."

All four of us piled into the police car. Two officers and I rode in the front seat, and Gebermedhin sat alone, in the back. The entire way to our destination, Gebermedhin was calling me filthy names and hurling insults.

We arrived in a very poor neighborhood, and I recognized the house of Gebermedhin's aunt. The second the car stopped I jumped out and they followed me into the house.

There was Yohannes! He was lying on a mat on the floor of the dark room. I rushed to my baby and cradled him in my arms. It felt so good to hold my son. But it didn't take long for me to notice how different my robust, cheerful child was. Yohannes was so skinny! And he smelled terrible! I was shocked and outraged when I learned that Gebermedhin's aunt had been feeding my son boiled mustard seeds. My chubby baby was thin, gaunt and lethargic. I held him and cried tears of joy and relief. And then I cried tears of roaring anger at the suffering my child had endured.

I sought the Lord and He answered me, and
rescued me from all my fears. (Psalm 34:4
NASB)

The police wanted me to go back to the police station and press charges against Gebermedhin. But I was so just so happy to have my baby back that all I wanted to do was to take Yohannes to the doctor to be examined.

The police persisted. "You must press charges," they said. "Your son might have died here."

"No," I cried tears of joy. "I don't want to take any time to press charges. Please, just take me to my baby's doctor."

The doctor examined Yohannes and prescribed a special diet to ease him back into proper nutrition. After being starved for nearly two months my baby needed extra care for the next four months. I thanked God over and over. Prior to the kidnapping, Yohannes was such a chubby baby. I'm sure it helped keep him alive.

Because I spent all my time looking for Yohannes, I lost my job at the Military base. But once I got Yohannes settled back into a routine at home with my servants, I was hired to work at the PX in retail. This provided good pay and excellent hours. I decided to keep the theater job since the children loved to go to the movies on Saturday and I could always use the extra cash.

I sought the Lord and He answered me, and
rescued me from all my fears. (Psalm 34:4
NASB)

PART 4

***

Meeting my American Cowboy Doctor

Things were going well with my job at the military base and the movie theatre. I liked being busy and I enjoyed making money and becoming financially solvent. The servants divided the duties in our tiny house. One looked after the children, and one took care of the meals, laundry and caring for the house. We were all getting along well and our tiny home was a happy, loving place. I was ready to buy a car or property where I could build a house.

And then I met an Air Force officer who changed my life. I know today that God put this man in my life to help me and my children leave Ethiopia.

It was a Friday night and I was attending a party at an officer's home on the base. There I met a dashing young Captain who looked like an American cowboy. He was so handsome, and I liked talking to him in English. The next week, he came through my check-out line at the PX. We chatted briefly and again I was struck by his boyish charm and handsome good looks. Then the following Saturday I saw him again when I took his ticket at the movie theatre.

"Hi!" he said with that shy smile I liked so much. "First, I see you at the party and then working at the PX. Why are you working here at the movie theatre too? You're young and so beautiful. Why are you working two jobs?"

I appreciated the compliment, but I didn't hesitate to explain. "Because I'm a single mother trying to support my three children by myself," I replied honestly.

We struck up a friendship after that. He told me about his impending divorce and the two children he had in the states. I told him about my disastrous marriage and struggle to make ends meet. He came to my house and met my children. He played with my kids and they liked him. As our relationship grew, we took my children places together. After nearly being arrested for kidnapping Yohannes, Gebermedhin was gone and no longer interested in the children, and they loved the attention of a father figure.

My cowboy Officer talked longingly about his own children and hoped to bring them to Ethiopia now that his divorce was final. We laughed at how much fun we imagined all five of our children would have playing together.

As our relationship grew, we began to make plans to marry. It would take a while to process all the paperwork for me to marry an American serviceman, and I was nervous and excited about blending my family culture with this handsome American. We planned to remain in Ethiopia where he was stationed for the next few years. After that I knew we would go wherever the Air Force assigned him.

I enjoyed the American friends I'd made at the base, and it was fun to be invited to so many social gatherings with my young cowboy Captain. I enjoyed getting dressed up and the Americans all accepted me into their social world. I was respected as an educated career woman, and I loved to hear about their world. Most of them came from the United States.

I will always remember that last party in Ethiopia. We were having drinks with several other officers and their wives, when the men received emergency call. Ethiopia had broken off all relations with the United States and all of the Americans had to leave the country immediately.

The Americans had three days to leave. My fiancé wanted me to leave Ethiopia with him. In the frantic fury of the mass exodus of the Americans, all of our friends were trying to help me leave with them. But it was impossible for me to be ready to leave in three days. The paperwork could never be prepared or processed in time.

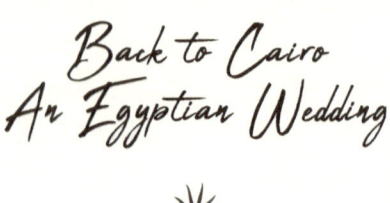

Back to Cairo
An Egyptian Wedding

After walking across the desert through Guerrilla infested war zones and escaping from my native country, it was decided that I would meet my American Captain in Cairo. We could be married there, but Egypt was primarily Islam and I didn't know what to do about where to be married. I didn't want to be married with Islam traditions. The simplest solution seemed to simply be married in a civil ceremony at city hall.

So, we took an agent from the American Embassy with us and we presented our paperwork, requesting to be married at Cairo city hall. We waited for hours as our agent went from one room back to another, then back to the other room, then back to the other, trying to process our marriage paperwork. For hours we watched him get up and go from one room to another and we didn't' know what was going on. Finally, we were called inside.

Each of us was asked, "What is your father's name? What is your mother's name?" Our answers were entered on a paper and then we were each asked to sign the paper.

I looked at the paper. It was written in Arabic. I had no idea what it said, but the agent assured me that by signing the paper, my American Captain and I would be married. So, both of us signed the Arabic document and we were pronounced husband and wife.

Becoming an American

We had a brief celebration with Dr. Watson and Judy and our friends in Cairo, and then we boarded a plane for Washington, DC. There we were greeted by all the US Air Force friends that knew us in Ethiopia. There was a big celebration at the airport.

We were going to stay with Christian friends who drove us to their home. I remember my first impressions of the United States. It was late in the afternoon, after 5 p.m. I was shocked to see trees in Washington, DC. I thought cities were the way they were depicted in the movies with concrete and skyscrapers. I was amazed at the beauty of the trees in the United States capital city.

I remember riding along staring up at the trees so happy to be in the United States. Everyone was chatting away when all of a sudden, a horrible smell filled the car. No one seemed to even notice but me. They kept driving and talking in loud, cheerful voices. The smell was so strong I could hardly breathe, but nobody in the car even seemed to notice it. I vividly recall being amazed by the trees and disturbed by the smell in confused emotion.

Eventually the smell disappeared, and as we continued down the road I kept looking up at the amazing trees.

That night we were all so excited. We had a wonderful dinner, and we were all talking and laughing together. I remember we were working together cleaning up the dinner dishes when I asked my friends, "What was that thing I was smelling in car?"

They all looked at me quizzically. "What smell?" they all asked.

I was so embarrassed. Everything was new to me and now it appeared that I should not have asked that question.

My first American culture experience was the next day when the girls decided to take me shopping. They wanted to buy me a coat, jacket, and boots. I was excited. I enjoyed fashion in Ethiopia, and here in the United States I imagined a beautiful leather jacket, a fur coat and high heel boots that went to my knees. I could hardly wait to be dressed by my American friends from American stores.

Our first stop was the shoe store where the girls wanted to buy my boots. I was so thrilled to be treated to their kindness and shopping trip, but I was surprised when they picked out rubber boots with soft fleece lining.

"Oh, these are great!" my friends explained. "See how soft they are inside. They'll be really warm."

I looked at the fleece-lined rubber boot with the flat heel. "This is not good!" I thought to myself. "What would I need this for? This is not for women!" I wanted high heels, and soft, supple leather. I didn't know what to say.

The salesman was an Ethiopian guy who introduced me to socks. I had never worn socks. I had worn nylon hose in Ethiopia when I was dressed up, but I had never worn socks. I was still embarrassed from my comments about the bad smell in the car and my fascination with the trees, so I just nodded agreement and my friends bought the boots.

From there we went to a large department store to purchase my new jacket. I headed toward the racks of leather jackets, dyed in beautiful colors, tanned with a soft buttery feel. But the girls took me to another part of the store where they picked out a thick puffy down ski jacket with a fleece lining.

I tried on the jacket, with its inflated arms and sides and thought, "What are they doing? They know my style back home, why did they pick this goofy looking jacket?"

The coat was a similar disappointment for me. I had envisioned a beautiful fur coat and instead they chose a heavy wool coat that felt like 20 pounds draped over my shoulders. I didn't express my confusion or disappointment, but I didn't understand that I would need all of these items for the cold winters ahead of me.

On the third day of our stay the girls decided to take me to New Jersey and New York for even more shopping. I was riding along in the car still fascinated by the trees when all of a sudden that smell came back into the car again. Everyone was chatting and laughing and again no one even skipped a beat when the foul smell filled the car.

Suddenly I couldn't help it, "Okay, everybody shut up!" I screamed. "This is the smell I was talking about! What is this smell? It's terrible! What is that awful smell?"

The girls erupted into a peel of laughter. "Oh AB," my friend explained. "It's a skunk!"

"A skunk?" I asked, dumbfounded at their casual attitude toward something that smelled so bad. "What is a skunk? We never have skunk in Ethiopia," I told them.

Then the girls explained to me what a skunk was and how they are often found along the roadside. I felt so much better and no longer embarrassed. The rest of the day was fun.

My fiancé was an Officer in the US Air Force, and he was stationed in Ohio. So soon we left Washington and headed for the Midwest. I was dazzled by the unexpected beauty and peacefulness of Ohio. This was a perfect place to bring my children.

Not only did Ohio have the same beautiful trees as Washington, but here I found vast farmland with pigs, horses, cows, and all sorts of American farm animals I didn't think that I would ever see. Our home was a large farmhouse on six acres with a big barn and lavish grounds. Every time I looked out over the pastures and watched my two stepchildren playing out there, I could imagine my three children running in the green grass, rolling down the hills, playing with the baby animals and living in the safety and security of the US. "Please God, help me to bring my children to this place," I prayed.

Therefore, I say to you, all things for which you pray and ask, believe that you have received them, and they will be granted to you. (Mark 11:24 NASB)

Our first order of business was to take our marriage certificate to Cincinnati for interpretation. The Ohio officials interpreted our marriage certificate, and I learned that in the first part of the Arabic document I was married to my husband, but on the bottom part of the document it stated that I was married to his father!

The easiest way to solve this was for us to be remarried. We went to the local Methodist church where I was greeted warmly. Instantly I found brothers and sisters in Christ through the church, and I felt so blessed by their friendship. It was 1977 and this was a dominantly white community, but no one seemed concerned about a bi-racial marriage or that I was from a third world country. Everyone was kind, loving and supportive as I became an American.

There is neither Jew nor Greek, there is neither slave nor free, there is neither male nor female; for you are all one in Christ Jesus. (Galatians 3:28 NASB)

The women of the church tried to teach me everything about the American culture. In Ethiopia I had servants who cooked and cleaned for me. Here I was learning to do it for my family. I had graduated from the home economics class in high school, so I had some background in taking care of a home, but no practical experience. These wonderful women taught me to cook. Every night someone would come over to teach me how to make different menu items. We had a new dish every night and even a new dessert each night. At least once a day, someone from the church came by to teach me something new about American culture.

The way these people invested their time in my American education was what saved me from despair. For even though I had two stepchildren to look after, I desperately missed my three children. I cried every single day, in fear and worry for my children. Sometimes my sobs were so fierce that I would wrap towels around me to fortify myself as I sobbed. I missed my kids, but the friendship of my new church family, made the pain bearable. I had one driving thought each day, and that was to bring my children out of Africa.

The US Air Force agreed to help me. The first thing I had to provide was birth certificates for my children. It took my friend in Addis Abeba, the capital city of Ethiopia, nine months to obtain birth certificates for me. That was nine months of agony. I worried about Johanas being so young, living with someone other than me. Would he even remember me? I worried about Liz and Sara. Were they safe at the Italian boarding school? Every night I had nightmares about my children. Were they safe? Were they alive? Would I ever see them again? "Please Father

God," I cried. "Watch over my children!" I was so fearful of the unknown. I had a passionate purpose in life during those days—simply to be with my children once again.

> *The Lord will protect you from all evil; He will keep your soul. The Lord will guard your going out and your coming in from this time and forever. (Psalm 121:7-8 NASB)*

Now I could plan to go get the birth certificates for my children. I was mentally ready to go back to Eritrea to get them. The only way I can explain how that day felt is to equate it with the same way I felt when I was spiritually born again. I felt so free and so very different.

I began processing to receive permission from Immigration to bring my children to the US. I knew what to expect this time and I had a better plan. This time my plan included walking shoes! I knew how dangerous the trip would be. I looked out at the quiet, serene pastures surrounding our home, and compared it to the war-torn country where my children were living. I had to get them out of there. I had to! Even if I died trying, I had to try to get my kids to safety. "Please, Father God. Help me!" I begged with each breath I took.

> *The eyes of the Lord are in every place, watching the evil and the good. (Proverbs 15:3 NASB)*

My husband and church family helped me prepare for the trip. Unlike my last trip, this time I had an air mattress for sleeping and proper supplies for the clandestine traveling. Dr. Watson wrote a letter to the American embassy in Eritrea advising them of my plan to kidnap my children and take them out of the country. It would be important to have the support of the American presence in Eritrea.

With US Immigration now on my side in my plan to bring my children to America, I corresponded with the Italian boarding school where Liz and Sara were staying. I had paid in advance for the girls to be at the boarding school for two years. I told them of my plan and that if they would help me get the girls out of Eritrea, they could keep whatever money was left over from what I had prepaid. I wrote to my uncle who was keeping Johanas, and he and the rest of the family were onboard with my plan. They were all ready to help me get my children out of Eritrea.

The plans of the heart belong to a person,
But the answer of the tongue is from the
Lord. (Proverbs 16:1 NASB)

***

PART 5

***

Rescuing My Children

❋

My American husband was not an overly emotional man. But the day before I left Ohio to go to New York to get my kids, he was tearful. He was so afraid for my safety and that I wouldn't come back.

Regretfully, he took me to the airport in Cincinnati to fly to New York. When he returned home, he sat down to read the newspaper. There was a headline about the war in Eritrea. The city of Asmara, my destination, had been bombed. The news story related that the civil war raging in Eritrea was worse than ever. Eritrea was a bad place to be right now.

I sat next to a friendly woman on the plane to New York and we discovered that we both had a four-hour layover in New York. Rather than sit in the airport, we decided to go shopping together during that time. When I returned to the airport, I heard my name being paged.

I responded to the page to find my husband on the phone. "AB, you must come home. The war in Eritrea is bad. It's all over the news," my husband pleaded. "It's very dangerous. You have to come back to Ohio. We'll figure something else out."

I sighed. I knew he was right. Eritrea was a dangerous place. But I knew with all my heart, that this was even more reason that I had to get my kids out of there.

"I'm not coming home," I told him. "If I'm going to die, I will die with my children," I said. And I hung up the phone. I realized at that moment that I was returning to Africa to rescue my children and I didn't know if they were even alive.

When I arrived in Eritrea, my first order of business was to visit the American embassy in Asklu. I shared my documents with them and tried to enlist their help. It didn't take long for me to figure out that the Americans were more interested in me for getting information for them from the field than in helping me rescue my children. I left my money with them for safekeeping and kept quiet about my plans. It did not appear that I would receive any real help from the Embassy.

Once again, I returned to Kasala. There I located a woman who was just kind of helping everybody. I explained my plan to get my kids.

She asked me, "Where are you from?"

"I am from the Hamasaid tribe," I told her.

"Who is your father?" She persisted.

I told her.

She brightened. "Your uncle is here!" she exclaimed. "He is the head of the Guerrilla fighters!"

My uncle was in Military conference at a closed meeting in Kasala at the very moment I arrived to rescue my children. Was it a coincidence or a stroke of luck? I didn't think so. I preferred to believe that there was God, unfolding his plan before me.

The woman sent my uncle a message. "Your niece is here from America."

A messenger brought a reply right back, "Keep her safe until I come out from the meeting."

I was so excited as I nervously waited for my uncle. I expected him any minute. "Please Father God," I prayed. "Keep the children safe and help us to be able to leave quickly."

I waited and waited for my uncle expecting his meeting to be over any minute. But he did not return. Three days later my uncle arrived from his meeting. I told him my plan.

"You stay here," he instructed.

"No way," I replied firmly.

We argued back and forth; him insisting that it was too dangerous for me to go out of the city and me insisting that I could not sit here and wait. I had to go after my kids. God was leading me to rescue them.

"I have to go!" I told him with a defiant look in my eye.

He fought me and I fought him back. "I can't stay, I have to go!" I implored him.

My uncle explained how very dangerous it was in that region, but I was relentless.

And so finally, he agreed to take me. I went with him the same way I came out of Asmara only this time I didn't have to walk. Since my uncle was the leader of the Guerrilla fighters, we traveled in a Military transport truck.

Slowly the truck rolled over the rubble of the war. The roads were often impassible and we would drive around many areas of debris and wreckage. But each mile brought me closer to my children until we were only about 40 miles away.

I sighed with anticipation. We were almost there. Only a little bit of travel left and I would see my children! And that's when the reality of the war roared into view. Suddenly there was major war activity with bombs blowing up around us and people dying in all directions. As the leader of the Guerrilla fighters my uncle had to stay and fight. He sent me back to Teseney, the opposite direction of my children. I was devastated.

My uncle sent me with a load of machine guns and military equipment and told the driver to take me to a home in Teseney. As the war raged on, I waited there for five days. It was safe and quiet there. There were no bombs going off, no sign of war, but the news was filled with reports of bombing in the city where my children lived. Over and over, I prayed, "Father God, please keep my children safe."

> *The Lord is good, A stronghold in the day of trouble, And He knows those who take refuge in Him. (Nahum 1:7 NASB)*

On the fifth day I decided that I needed to go into the city. Facing the bombing I located the woman who had helped me find my uncle and asked her to help me find someone to take me to my children. Two days later I contracted a man who would take me to my children and bring us back for a small fee of about $30.

Together, this man and I planned that our trip would start late in the afternoon. We would have to walk at night. I looked at my appearance. My hair was straight and styled, my nails manicured and polished. After living in the United States for nine months, I no longer looked like a refugee or a native Ethiopian. My skin wasn't drawn and dry. My eyes weren't sunken, and I knew that I would be taking a big risk if I ventured out like this. So to be safe, we boiled water with salt and I washed my face with the salt water and let it air dry. This changed the texture of my complexion.

My friend cut my nails and then proceeded to braid my hair into tight corn rows, a traditional African style. I had never braided my hair before, and I feared that the braids would be tight and uncomfortable. She had just started braiding my hair with one little row down the very center of my head. I vividly recall that I was wearing a light, transparent sleeping gown. Just as she started making a second braid, my uncle walked in. He was startled at how different I now looked.

Before he could say a word, I begged him, "Where are my kids?" And before he could answer, I fainted.

When I came to, I got up with grief and pain, and I asked in desperation once again, "Uncle, where are my children?" I was so fearful of the answer. Had they died in a bombing?

"Your kids are at the hotel," he answered with a twinkle in his eye.

Hallelujah! I just jumped up and ran right out into the middle of the street. I was deliriously happy that my children were right here, and I ran about a quarter of a mile down the street before I realized that I didn't know where I was going or that I was wearing a see-through night gown that was totally inappropriate to wear in public. None of that mattered—my children were alive, and I was going to see them!

My uncle and friend had followed me outside, and they caught up to me in my hysteria.

"Where are they?" I begged. "Where are they?" I was desperate to see my beautiful, precious children.

"What is your problem?" my uncle laughed. "Your kids are fine, they're at the hotel."

"I just want my kids," I told him. "I just want my kids! Please take me to them."

He took me to the hotel where Johanas, Liz, Sara and I had a joyful reunion. I held them tenderly in my arms and the tears poured out of my eyes. I rocked them back and forth and whispered how much I had missed them. I thanked God over and over that I was reunited with these precious babies that filled my heart so dearly. After nine months of being separated in a war zone, it was an amazing moment. God had led us through this ordeal this far, and I felt comfort in His grace to get us through the rest of the journey.

"Thank you, God." I prayed. "Thank you."

Rejoice always, pray without ceasing, in everything give thanks; for this is the will of God for you in Christ Jesus. (1 Thessalonians 5:16-18 NASB)

"We have to celebrate!" I told my hostess. So, I bought a whole lamb and her entire neighborhood helped me celebrate with a feast.

The next day, I told my uncle, "We have to go."

He argued, "No, we cannot go yet. I have some important work to do here first. I will take you as soon as I can."

I nagged him. "No uncle, we must go!" I begged and pleaded. "We must go! I cannot risk keeping the children here. I need to get them to a safer place."

"There is no fighting here!" my uncle argued. "In a few days I will take you."

"No!" I insisted. "We must go now!"

I would not give him any peace, and finally after hours of arguing he gave in. He was so angry with me, but he agreed to take us as soon as night fell the following day.

And true to his word, my uncle, my children and I, along with a small entourage of fighters left in a Military transport truck at nightfall. Yohannes, Liz, Sara, and I sat in the back of the truck on top of the cargo. The children were fearful, and I tried to encourage them.

"Mama is here," I whispered to them, "I'm not leaving you ever again."

We traveled all night on the truck and at daylight the driver pulled the truck under the cover of trees where we slept in the back of the truck. It was far too dangerous for us to travel during the day for any vehicle on the road was a target for the airplane Bombers. The roads and debris along the way were a testament to the destruction that had happened before us along this path.

Yohannes was barely four and he was so excited to be on our trip. At his young age, he was already brainwashed for war.

"Mama," he explained to me with all sincerely, "The Eritreans have machine guns! We can blow up the enemy. We can shoot for freedom!"

"Father God, help me to get him out of here and to our safe farm in Ohio." I prayed.

On the second day, Sara became ill. She started throwing up anything she ate. I worried. It could just be from the motion of the truck or the dust, but what if it was Malaria? With every bump along the way I prayed that God would keep the children safe.

I told the children about our farm in Ohio. I tried to describe the trees, the green grass, the animals and our big farm house. I told them about their step-brother and step-sister and how eager my husband's children were to meet them. It was hard to keep the kids encouraged with the dangers of the war all around us, but I did my best to remain cheerful and optimistic. I could barely stop hugging them.

It was the second night along the road when another Military transport truck pulled up beside us and the driver announced that Teseney had been bombed. The woman who had hosted me was killed in the bombings. I shivered as I learned the news of her fate, for I knew without a doubt, that God had spared our lives once more.

"Thank you for your protection, Father," I said in a whisper. "Please keep these children in your care."

> *My God, my rock, in whom I take refuge, My shield and the horn of my salvation, my stronghold and my refuge; My savior, You save me from violence. I call upon the Lord, who is worthy to be praised, And I am saved from my enemies. (2 Samuel 22:3-4 NASB)*

The third day we came to the next town and just after we had moved on, another bombing occurred in that town. As I watched the war unfold, it seemed as if the Bombers were following us, bombing places right after we left there. But the reality was that the war was just getting worse and worse.

When we neared the border of Sudan and Eritrea it was in the very early morning hours before the sun came up. Because we were with the Guerilla fighters, we were able to stay in a hotel-like home.

The sun had just risen when we heard the alarm bell clanging to warn us of an approaching Bomber. I grabbed the children and we all scurried out into the night down

127

into an underground bomb shelter. We sat there waiting, petrified of what was to come. The children were terrified, crying and holding on to me. I tried to comfort them in the dark bunker and silently prayed that God would once again protect us.

> But the Lord is faithful, and He will strengthen and protect you from the evil one. (2 Thessalonians 3:3 NASB)

We waited and waited, but no bombs were dropped. My uncle instructed me to get the children dressed, to pack and be ready to leave as quickly as possible. We only had 17 miles to go to Kassala, the capital city of Sudan and the Bombers would not bomb that close to the Sudanese.

With only seventeen miles to reach to Kassala we dared to venture out in the daylight. We arrived unscathed but exhausted from the tension of the danger that loomed in our midst. At Kassala I was able to obtain the necessary vaccinations for the children to travel. Not stopping to visit with any of the friends or family in the area we set out to Khartoum and then on to Egypt.

Flight to New York

The flight from Cairo to New York is especially memorable. The three children and I were in a big jet seated together in a middle row. The girls, ages seven and eight, were wiggly and excited, but Yohannes, only four, was so active and talked non-stop. He didn't speak English, but he jabbered away at the guy next to us in our native Ethiopian language.

"My mother bought this plane," he told the man importantly. "She bought it for us to go to go to America." He nodded his head, his big brown eyes sparkling.

"Is that right?" The man asked in English not understanding anything Johanas had said.

"Yes!" Yohannes answered back, as if he understood English. "We are going to America and Mama bought this plane for us!"

Sara had left her best friend behind at the boarding school. The mother of Sara's friend had forgotten her child at the Italian boarding school. Sara begged me to go back and get her friend.

"Please, Mama, please. We can't leave her there!" Sara begged. At age seven, Sara didn't understand all the paperwork and government regulations that would prevent me from being able to bring her friend to the United States.

Liz was more reflective on the trip watching everything with big bright eyes, just taking it all in. She was excited to begin her new life, but she was also eager to tell me about her boarding school experience. It made me feel good to know that she had been well cared for in my absence.

When our plane landed in the United States, I was consumed with a joy I had never before experienced. My children were now safe in America—the land of freedom and opportunity. My children would grow up in a safe community with parents who loved them, in a society that valued them, and they would be able to develop their God-given talents and gifts. The tears that filled my eyes washed the terror from my heart.

> *I will give thanks to the Lord according to His righteousness And will sing praise to the name of the Lord Most High. (Psalm 7:17 NASB)*

When we arrived back home in Ohio, the church family embraced my children and took an active role in teaching them about America. My two stepchildren welcomed Yohannes, Sara and Liz into their home, and we began the process of the children's Americanization.

Harriett Bennett was a teacher at the local school. She helped my children learn and adjust to the new language and culture. My husband and I spoke English at home and soon the children were speaking it well. Yohannes especially caught on to the English language, and even picked it up with an American accent. Between church, school, and our Mormon neighbors with eight kids next door, my children were surrounded by a loving community and relaxed into the peaceful valley of Ohio.

It wasn't all easy. My stepchildren accepted my kids, but they didn't accept me. I had spent my parenting life just trying to keep my children safe and to provide for their primary needs. I didn't know anything about how to provide emotional support, or that our family might have benefited from family counseling. I was so naïve and to this day I regret that I wasn't able to better help my stepchildren as we blended our families.

My husband's children were so special. My stepdaughter was a sweet little girl and my young step-son was so kind and funny. I love them both dearly, but I have regrets about our rocky start as a family. I am grateful that today we are very close.

California Here We Come!

As much as I loved living in America, I detested the cold winters of Ohio. I learned to bundle up on the cold mornings and to build a fire in the fireplace for added warmth. But I just couldn't see the beauty of the snow or enjoy the frigid outdoors of mid-Western winters.

One day I was standing in the kitchen of my big farmhouse, cooking dinner, when I heard a loud explosion in the basement. I opened the door to the basement and there was smoke coming up the steps. I called for my husband, but he had left for work already, so I called the fire department.

I didn't appear to be in any danger, so I just kept cooking dinner.

The firemen showed up, sirens blaring, in a bright red truck and came bounding up the front porch. I opened the door and one of them asked, "Are you okay?"

I wiped my hands on my apron and answered, "Yes, I think so. The fire is downstairs."

I led them through the house into the kitchen and turned off the burner. I opened the basement door, and the firemen descended the steps to check out the explosion.

"I think you should wait outside," the fireman said as he headed into the basement.

The firemen returned from the basement to announce that our furnace had exploded. I called my husband with the news, and he called Sears to come out and bring us a new furnace the next day. I wasn't sure how we were going to make it through the night with no heat, but I thought we could probably manage a camp-out in front of the fireplace with the kids for one night.

The next morning, instead of Sears, we welcomed a tornado. This was a whole new kind of cold; a cold that I had never experienced before. It was so cold in our farmhouse that we burned two cords of wood in the fireplace trying to keep warm. We all sat by the fireplace wrapped up in layers of clothing and extra blankets. It was too cold to cook and people from the church brought us food and an electric heater. For three days we were without our furnace and due to the storm, there was no school, so we were trying to entertain the kids in the subzero temperature of the house.

My husband was from California, and he told my children about the great weather there. "It's warm this time of year," he explained. "It hardly ever freezes and never snows."

"Let's move there!" Yohannes said. "I could learn to surf!"

It was so cold in that house that I would have been willing to move anywhere in the United States if the temperature was above freezing.

One day while we were driving to the Air Force Base, I saw a sign that said, "Veterinary Clinic."

"What kind of research do they do there?" I asked my husband.

"What do you mean?" He asked. "I don't think they do any research there."

Why would there be a Veterinary Clinic there, then?" I asked.

My husband explained. "It's an animal hospital. That's what most Veterinarians do. Treat animals."

"An animal hospital? For dogs and cats?" I asked in disbelief. "How are those Veterinarians different than you?"

"They have the same medical degree," he explained. "I'm a Veterinarian who does research for the US Air Force."

"What do they do there?" I persisted.

"People bring their pets there if the animals get sick or need procedures," he patiently answered.

"You're serious?" I asked incredulously. "Dogs and cats have their own medical clinic? Their own doctor?"

"Yes, AB," my husband grinned. "Veterinarians make a pretty good living if they have an established practice."

He pulled into the parking lot of the Veterinary Clinic and after showing his credentials and explaining my interest in veterinary medicine, we were able to take a tour of the facility. I saw an exam room, the surgery, the treatment rooms, and it was much nicer than most medical clinics in Ethiopia. It looked just like a hospital.

"You are serious?" I asked again. "People in America pay money to have their animals treated by a doctor?" It was a concept I had not ever considered before.

"Yes, Veterinarians are respected medical professionals in the United States," my husband was grinning again.

"Are you qualified to work in a place like this?" I asked.

"Sure," he replied. "But the Air Force pays me to do research, not treat pets."

"Unbelievable!" I explained. I was so fired up. I had grown up working in an understaffed, outdated medical clinic for a population that desperately needed proper medical care. Now I discovered that in America pets were given far better medical care than my father was able to provide for people in my homeland.

"Can you resign from the Air Force?" I asked. My mind was buzzing with the possibility of my husband having his own Veterinary Clinic.

"I could," my husband conceded.

"What are you doing working for the Air Force?" I asked. "Let's open our own Veterinary Clinic!"

That afternoon my husband resigned his commission with the US Air Force and in a few weeks, we bundled our family up and moved to Northern California. He began his first job treating animals as an associate veterinarian at a clinic in a rural community. While he enjoyed the work with the animals, it wasn't too long before we wanted to have our own practice.

"It will take money," he warned.

"So, we'll sell one of our cars," I said. "We can do this. You will be a great doctor and people will want to bring their pets to your hospital," I told him with pride.

My husband's parents gave us a small loan to open our own animal hospital in a nearby community. We opened a clinic in the downstairs of a home near the local college with used equipment and lots of enthusiasm.

Opening a business, with our home above it, created more problems than we anticipated. There were all sorts of codes the city made us adhere to. One was about having enough parking spaces for our clients. The cost of paving the parking lot was out of the question for us, so I had a load of gravel dumped in the lot, and each day, while my husband was in surgery, I would spread a few wheelbarrows of gravel around the parking lot. During lunch time, we would both do a few loads until we had completed the entire lot.

My husband was the doctor, and I was the receptionist, veterinary tech, accountant, kennel cleaner, wife, and mother. We lived upstairs with all the kids, and it was such a good time.

By this time our son Isaac was born and we were a family of seven, living above the animal hospital. My husband's daughter had gone to live with her mother, but Scott, my step-son remained with our blended family. There was a lot of fun and laughter in our house, and

I loved my husband with all my heart. He was a kind, gentle person, a great father to my children and was providing well for our family with his veterinary practice.

I loved Northern California with its sunshine and warm winters. And I enjoyed the little community where we lived. The children attended a nearly all-white school, but they were accepted and included socially. It didn't ever occur to me that being thrust into a "white bread" community might be challenging for them. Everywhere I went in our community I was greeted warmly and welcomed.

I was raising the all-American family. I learned to be a Room Mother and to chaperone Scouts. I drove kids to soccer, basketball, football, and swimming practice. I became involved in school, community, service clubs and church. The real estate agent who had sold us the animal hospital invited us to her Mormon Church, so we began instruction for the Mormon Church membership. Things were going well there, until the final week of the classes when a video explained about the history of the Mormon Church, extolling the virtues of their founder, and discounting the divinity of Jesus. I walked out and I've never been back. Our family found a Christian church and continued to worship Jesus as the son of God.

And the Word became flesh, and dwelt among us; and we saw His glory, glory as of the only Son from the Father, full of grace and truth. (John 1:14 NASB)

The animal hospital was doing very well financially, and in a few years my husband and I were able to build our dream home just a few miles from the clinic. I had also purchased a small café and that business was off to a good start. Our children were doing well in school, graduating from a top college prep high school and moving on to college and careers. Both my husband and I were active in our local Chamber of Commerce and our church.

In 1992 the veterinary practice received an award from the Chamber of Commerce. I was flattered and humbled by my husband's acceptance of the award when he credited me for the success of our business. My heart swelled with pride at his achievement and for being part of his success.

And God is able to make all grace overflow to you, so that, always having all sufficiency in everything, you may have an abundance for every good deed. (2 Corinthians 9:8 NASB)

The End of a Fairy Tale

Shortly after receiving the Chamber of Commerce award, my husband explained to me that after 17 years he was leaving our marriage. He had met a young woman with small children and no longer wanted to be married to me.

I was shocked beyond belief. My husband moved out of our dream home back to the apartment above our animal clinic, but not before he cleaned out all of our bank accounts and cancelled all of my credit cards.

My heart was broken, and I didn't know what to do. I was left with the mortgage on our big house and property, and no money to pay the electric bill or to buy groceries. My little café was supporting itself, but there was no money to take out for profit just yet. I had nothing. Our three oldest children were grown, but equally distraught over the dissolution of their family. And each of them suffered differently. Johanas ran away from our family. Sarah became distant. Liz tried to pretend it wasn't happening and Isaac, the only child still living at home, was extremely confused and angry. The children vacillated between supporting me and blaming me for their father's abandonment, for when my husband walked out on me, he left the children as well.

I clung to the promises of God, but I wondered how I was going to navigate this mess. The electricity was turned off in our big house when I couldn't pay the bill. This was a rural location and being without electric service to the house also meant there was no electrical power for the pump for our well. Not only was I without lights, I was without water. I sat in the dark at night and showered at a friend's house the next morning. The mortgage foreclosed and I received notice to vacate the premises.

In my grief and despair, I tried to form a plan and I decided that I would pack a few things and sleep in my car. I decided that I would park the car near the church where I would be safe. I had packed some, but not all of our household items since I didn't have anywhere to take them, and I couldn't afford storage. Isaac had moved in with his father, and all I had left to care for was myself. I felt so alone, yet sustained in my faith that God would somehow provide.

"Father God," I prayed. "Please help me through this bleak desert."

> *"Because of the devastation of the poor, because of the groaning of the needy, Now I will arise," says the Lord; "I will put him in the safety for which he longs." (Psalm 12:5 NASB)*

I remember sitting in my dark house all alone, trying to gather my courage to get in the car and drive to the church to spend the night, when I looked up and noticed that several cars were coming down our private driveway. I was sure they were coming from the mortgage company to evict me. But instead, they were people from my church, and friends in the community.

"What are you all doing here?" I asked them at the door, in wonder.

"We're here to help," my friend said pushing past me and walking into the house.

"But how can you help?" I asked. "I don't have anywhere to go?"

"Yes, you do!" she laughed. More people came into the house and began packing up boxes and taking furniture out to their pickups and cars.

My friend had rented a house for me and she had mobilized this group to pack me up and help me move. Within hours they moved me into a rented home with electricity, warm running water and a stocked refrigerator. I felt so blessed and overwhelmed with God's answer to my prayer.

> *Consider the ravens, that they neither sow nor reap; they have no storeroom nor barn, and yet God feeds them; how much more valuable you are than the birds! (Luke 12:24 NASB)*

The divorce was a bitter battle between legal counsels. I learned from friends and my lawyer that part of the veterinary clinic belonged to me. This was definitely different than Ethiopian culture, but I didn't approach this American law with greed. I just wanted to have a fair share of the business to start over again to support Isaac and myself. I felt confident in my entrepreneurial skills, but I did need some collateral to get started.

My husband, who had always been so generous and giving, wanted me to keep my little café and to keep the clinic for himself. My café was just a fledging restaurant, while the clinic was a respected business and was doing very well financially. Then my husband began to misrepresent how the clinic was doing financially. I was able to prove otherwise by waiting until he left the clinic and making copies of documents. The business wasn't doing as well as when we had been running it together, but it was still making money.

Lawyers cost money and my lawyer wanted a lot of money. It didn't take long and my lawyer needed more money to fight for me in the divorce settlement. And I didn't have it. One day a friend and her husband from Rotary Club dropped by to chat. "What do you need today, AB?" my friend asked.

"Nothing," I smiled bravely. "I'm doing okay."

My friend's husband frowned, "No, I think maybe you need our help. What do you need?"

"Come, AB," my friend encouraged. "What's going on? What can we help you with today?"

I laughed. "Oh, my lawyer just wants another $10,000 and I don't have $10 to give him."

"We'll take care of it," her husband replied. And just like that, they helped me. They didn't ask any questions. They didn't want repayment; they just helped me. I was amazed at how God showed me His love through these friends.

> But seek first His kingdom and His righteousness, and all these things will be provided to you. (Matthew 6:33)

After three years the divorce trial was set for September 26, 1995. But that was the day of the O.J. Simpson verdict, and our court date was postponed. My lawyer didn't want me to accept the new date offered because the judge who was scheduled for the new date did not have a history of being sympathetic to wives.

"Don't take this date, AB," he advised. "We'll ask for a different date."

I was exhausted and just wanted it over. By now I didn't even care who got what. It looked to me like the lawyers were the only winners in this battle.

"No!" I insisted. "We will go with the new date. I'm not waiting any longer."

Our trial was held a few weeks later and a decree was finally granted. I was shocked when the judge awarded the clinic and the café to me. This wasn't even what I had petitioned for. This was far more than I wanted.

I expected the news to rock our little town. Both my ex-husband and I had been active in so many social organizations, clubs, activities, and we had so many mutual friends; I didn't know what kind of reaction to expect from all of them.

But the community supported me. I was especially gratified by the support and encouragement and even congratulations I received from many of the men in our town. But even with all this support, I still didn't want to keep the clinic. It had gone from representing such a joyful, jubilant time in my life to total devastation that I didn't want to hold on to it.

However, I did move back into the clinic apartment, and began to rebuild the business. Here I drew my strength from God as I watched him put a multitude of friends on my path to help me rebuild my life. And as He did, I began to heal from all the wounds the divorce had inflicted.

It was during this time that I discovered something about finding God's peace. I prayed daily that God would give me wisdom, help me work out my problems, and to give me His peace. As I struggled through the aftermath of the divorce, I learned that the peace of God is not the absence of a problem. But within the problem is where I could find God's peace for His presence was there.

> *You keep him in perfect peace whose mind is stayed on You, because he trusts in You. (Isaiah 26:3 ESV)*

Casualties of Divorce

The failure of my marriage was very difficult on all of the children. Yohannes ran away and Sara became so angry she was unable to cope. She blamed me for the divorce and refused to even talk to me about it. This broke my heart all over again. Over and over I prayed that God would restore my family. I kept praying that my relationship with Sara would mend. Each day I would lift Sara up to God and ask for His help and then I would take the problem back and try to solve it myself. Every one of my attempts to reconcile with Sara was rebuffed.

One day in desperation I lifted Sara before the Lord and said, "Father God, Sara is your child. Please watch over her and protect her, and if there is a way for us to be mother and daughter again, please make it so. I'm done trying to do this myself." And I left Sara on an imaginary "altar" before God.

Sara called me the next day. She needed my help and gently asked if I could assist her. I was so surprised I wondered if it was really Sara on the other end of the phone line. And then it occurred to me that by completely giving Sara to God and not meddling in His plan for Sara God was able to answer my prayer.

Psalm 55:22 NASB Cast your burden upon the LORD and He will sustain you;

He will never allow the righteous to be shaken.

Isaac was the only child still living at home when his father wanted out of our marriage. He was just entering his teen years and having his world turned upside down was more than Isaac could handle. Bouncing back and forth between his father and I was extremely confusing and difficult for him. Like many teens in the American culture Isaac found comfort in illegal drugs.

The drugs lead Isaac down a deadly, dangerous path that was more treacherous than anything Sara, Liz or Yohannes had ever experienced in Ethiopia. Here in America, the land of freedom and opportunity, my beautiful, intelligent, vibrant son, born an American, was a slave to chemical dependency. It went from simply skipping school, to breaking the law, to being arrested, to being housed in juvenile hall.

My heart had already been broken by the dissolution of my marriage to his father, but nothing prepared me for the heartache and desperation I felt when I watched the policemen handcuff my young son, put him in a squad car and take him to jail. I prayed with every breath I took, that God would help me help my son.

I was introduced to "tough love." It's a tactic taught in parenting classes of juveniles in the justice system. What

I learned is that using "tough love" is tougher on parents than teens.

Isaac defiantly refused to adhere to the curfews that I set. He would show up late no matter what the curfew time was. The counselor told me that I had to be firm about the results of breaking my curfew rules. So I agreed to try it. My heart shattered when Isaac was 15 minutes late and I locked the door. When he arrived, he knocked on the door, and I didn't let him in.

"Mom!" Isaac called. "It's me, Isaac. Let me in!"

I didn't answer.

"Mom!" Isaac called. "It's me. Let me in."

I didn't go to the door. I stayed in my room, praying that God would help us. "Father God, please give me wisdom and courage to follow it," I prayed through my tears.

"Mom!" Isaac continued to call. For over an hour, this little tap, tap, tap, on the door would nudge my conscience. A weary, sad voice would call, "Mom, It's me. Your son, Isaac. Please, let me in."

Isaac slept on the concrete step outside the front door that night. And it rained.

I will never forget sobbing in my bedroom, wrapped in the warmth of a soft quilt, pleading with God to give me the strength to practice this tough love; and begging God to forgive me for leaving my baby to sleep out in the rain.

*He who withholds his rod hates his son, But
he who loves him disciplines him diligently.
(Proverbs 13:24 NASB)*

As Isaac progressed through high school the drugs made him unable to concentrate. Drug addiction took over his mind, his heart and his motivation. It seemed like Isaac was either in juvenile hall or rehab. When Isaac turned seventeen, I knew that I had less than a year to get help for him for once he turned eighteen, I could no longer force him into treatment.

I found an inpatient treatment center in Napa, California that would take Isaac. They had remarkable success with teen addicts, but it was extremely expensive. Family and friends, community members, church members and people I didn't even know, helped me.

Less than a year later Isaac graduated from high school at the treatment center as class Valedictorian. During his speech he gave me credit for his success. I thought about all the tough love I had managed with my handsome son. I looked at his cheerful face, his beautiful dark eyes sparkling again, his disposition and attitude so fresh. I felt waves of relief wash over me. Isaac's transformation was incredible. It was a miracle to see my son restored to what God had created. I was so proud of Isaac's victorious battle and that he was able to complete his education as well. God had truly answered my prayers and my son was on the right track to reaching his potential. Isaac was happy, healthy and even his countenance was peaceful. Once again God had answered my prayers.

> *The Lord cause His face to shine on you, And be gracious to you; The Lord lift up His face to you, And give you peace. (Numbers 6:25-27 NASB)*

Upon graduation and release from the program Isaac was reluctant to come back home. He wanted to make a fresh start and decided to move to Los Angeles with his older brother, Yohannes. Today Isaac is happy, healthy, and going to college. He is now an amazing father, and I am so proud of him. I thank God every day for giving me the courage to help Isaac fight drug addiction.

> *"For I know the plans that I have for you," declares the Lord, "plans for prosperity and not for disaster, to give you a future and a hope." (Jeremiah 29:11 NASB)*

Recovering from Heartbreak

Recovering from a bitter divorce is a slow process. Through prayer, and the support of my family and friends I overcame the grief. The Lord continued to put people in my life who reached out to help me. People I didn't even know helped pay for counseling, and my relationship with God deepened. It took a while, but soon I was noticeably happier and my joy returned.

I continued to study my Bible and gleaned wisdom from God through the pages of His word. One day I was reading a scripture in Isaiah and I felt like the words were speaking directly to my heart.

> *I make known the end from the beginning, from ancient times, what is still to come. I say: My purpose will stand, and I will do all that I please. From the east I summon a bird of prey; from a far-off land, a man to fulfill my purpose. What I have said, that will I bring about; what I have planned, that will I do. (Isaiah 46:10-11 NIV)*

I thought about how God had brought me from a far-off land and I wanted to fulfill His purpose in my life. And I decided to become more involved in ministry.

I wanted to go back to my life-long devotion of helping others. I began a small ministry for women we called "Heart to Heart." We met once a month in my café for a Bible study and support group for women. In no time our group grew to a minister to over 900 women, all hurting and looking to God for healing.

As I began to help others heal, my healing became more powerful. I learned to completely depend on God for everything. When I looked back at my life, in the earlier years of my marriage, I remembered the joy and feeling that I had everything—a good marriage, healthy, happy children, a big house, a successful business, respect in the community—and then it all crumbled and I had nothing.

> *He said, "Naked I came from my mother's womb, And naked I shall return there. The Lord gave and the Lord has taken away. Blessed be the name of the Lord." (Job 1:21 NASB)*

Now I was trying to rebuild my life and I was older. I had no one to be my partner except God. More than once, I thought that this was worse than any challenge I had faced before—even worse than crossing a war infested desert. For a while I considered going back home and just running away from this place that brought me so much pain.

But the Lord was so good to me and He reminded me that he had provided me with dozens of people in the United States who became my sisters. As I reflected on how the women had helped me those first few days in America, taking me shopping and explaining basic American traditions to me, I thanked God. I remembered Harriett in Ohio who "Americanized" me and answered all my dumb questions patiently and kindly. God reminded me about all the people in my little town in California who moved me out of my cold, dark house into a warm apartment, who painted my clinic before I moved back in, or put down new carpet in the apartment before I returned, or paid for my counseling, and I was fortified with how God continued to bless me in my despair.

> *And not only this, but we also celebrate in our tribulations, knowing that tribulation brings about perseverance; and perseverance, proven character; and proven character, hope; and hope does not disappoint, because the love of God has been poured out within our hearts through the Holy Spirit who was given to us. (Romans 5:3-4 NASB)*

I started listening more closely to God. I read my scriptures and prayed daily. I prayed for the veterinary business asking God to bless it according to His purpose.

It kept me going. I didn't know why or how. I knew I wasn't anyone special. I wasn't different and I knew that lots of other people had gone through similar life challenges. But the way God showed me His love to me through all this conflict and resolution, and as I reflected on the kindness shown to me by God's people, each of them became amazing to me.

But my healing was fraught with doubt and despair. As I watched my husband remove himself from our family, my pain expanded to cover the grief of the children as well as my own. Not only did I no longer have my home, income or love of a man I truly loved, but I was watching my children endure similar pain.

I remember sitting in my bedroom and crying, so upset with God for taking me through this dark valley of grief. I could feel God tugging at my heart, but I stubbornly refused to be comforted. Boldly I told God, "I'm not going to talk to you until you answer all my questions."

"Why? Why, God?" I asked Him. "I was a good wife. I was a good mother. I worked hard to build up a good business for him. Why did you let it all crumble?"

I wiped my eyes and looked up, continuing my tirade. "I'm not asking for anything extravagant. "I just need to pay my bills. I don't even have money to buy a few groceries, and he's out going dancing every night. He's got money and he's doing all this destruction to our family!"

I sat there alone, determined that I wouldn't move until God answered me. Tears were pouring down my face, as I sat on the bed with my arms crossed in defiance. My anger was focused completely on me and my pain.

"I'm not moving until you answer me," I said flatly.

Out of nowhere I heard a soft question, "Can you see his pain?"

I looked around annoyed. "What pain?" I threw my arms into the air and asked. I folded my arms around myself again.

"Can you see his pain?" The quiet question came again.

During this tirade the phone rang a few times, and I heard knocks at my door. I refused to answer either determined to get some kind of answer from the God that I knew loved me, but He seemed to be taking a calloused approach to my pain.

"What pain?" I asked again wanting an answer from God.

"He does not have Me to get him through his pain," I heard God say.

Suddenly I realized how selfish I had been. And I did see my husband's pain. And I became sorry for his pain as well as my own. Although there was no hope of reconciliation of the marriage, I did still love him, and I didn't want him to be hurting.

With this revelation I was in a different place. I was totally different and instead of crying for my grief, I was crying for his salvation, for his life, and for forgiveness for him.

Psalm 119:32 I shall run the way of Your command-ments, for You will enlarge my heart.

I couldn't sleep, so I started moving furniture and cleaning the house. About 11:30 p.m. the phone rang again and this time I answered. It was my neighbors and friends who were just checking in with me.

"Hi AB," my friend said. "We just want you to know we are praying for you." I saw again that God loves me with the kindness of friends. God spoke to me through them right at the moment when my heart was thirsty to hear it. I felt so much peace. I just went to bed, relaxing in the comfort of God showing me His love.

John 16:33 NASB These things I have spoken to you so that in Me you may have peace. In the world you have tribulation, but take courage; I have overcome the world."

From this event, everything changed. The Lord start-ed talking to me although I suspect He had been speak-ing to me all along, but I wasn't listening before. "Go and ask him to forgive you," God told me one day.

I was stunned. I didn't do anything wrong. He cheat-ed on me! Before I would have argued with God; but, I chose to be obedient to God and traveled to find my husband and asked him for forgiveness. It wasn't a good meeting, but it didn't matter to me. I had followed God's direction and felt at peace. There were other meetings later when he wanted to try to reconcile, but I knew that God had taken me through all this pain toward His will for me and declined all offers.

For if you forgive other people for their offenses, your heavenly Father will also forgive you. But if you do not forgive other people, then your Father will not forgive your offenses. (Matthew 6:14-15 NASB)

I had come to believe that everything was about the heart being in the right place. No matter what happens to us, the truth sets us free. I was experiencing a trusting time with God.

If the Son sets you free, you will be free indeed. (John 8:36 NIV)

Once the clinic became mine, I began to rebuild the practice. Each day I would go around the property and pray for God to make the business succeed. Before long, life started being good again. I interviewed several Veterinarians for the clinic. I was able to settle on hiring a young woman Veterinarian, but she wasn't able to start work immediately.

Different Veterinarians from nearby communities called and offered to work in my clinic until she could arrive. They covered the hospital and emergency care needs until the new Vet could take over. Without a licensed Vet on staff, I was unable to order veterinary drugs. These veterinarians stepped in and ordered for me through their offices.

Through it all, the Lord was good. Business was way down and the girls working there were looking for another job since they didn't know how long I could stay open. I continued to pray and trust God and before long business increased. And once again, God showed His love to me.

There was also an internal struggle for me by moving back into the clinic apartment where we had first begun our practice. There was a great deal of pain moving into that place. As grateful as I was that I had a house, it was hard to be in a home where we had loved and lived as such a happy family. I often felt two spirits tugging at me—a spirit of light and a spirit of darkness. But I had faith that the light would win over the dark. And even as the clinic began earning more money, I felt the pain of living there was distracting me.

There were so many things that needed upgrading or repair, and new equipment we needed to buy, that I couldn't afford. I also felt compelled to pay a court ordered $50,000 to my ex-husband in a lump sum instead of monthly payments. I had applied for a loan, but I knew no one would loan me any money. I didn't have any collateral except the clinic and my credit was ruined by the divorce. I realized that I didn't want to be in this business anymore and I made the decision to sell the clinic. I just wanted to get out.

I put the clinic on the market. It represented a dream we'd had together and I couldn't be part of it anymore. I found a corporate buyer and I took the offer home to review one night. I looked it all over and prayed about it carefully.

I decided that I didn't like this offer and thought that I would submit a counter offer. I prepared to go to the Realtor's office the next morning and in my morning Bible study the Lord gave me a Bible verse from Joshua:

Joshua 10:25 NASB Joshua then said to them, "Do not fear or be dismayed! Be strong and courageous, for the Lord will do this to all your enemies with whom you fight."

The phone rang and what seemed to be out of nowhere, the Lord provided a bank loan for me.

I was shocked. "How did you do that?" I asked the woman on the phone.

The loan officer explained that occasionally they can make exceptions to their policies and my check was ready for me to pick up. This was a direct gift from God. So, I re-read the message from Joshua 10:25 again and followed the Lord's direction. I cancelled the sale. I took care of my employees and business was booming. I hired more staff and within a couple years returned the business to the same financial stability I had enjoyed before. And then, when God told me it was time, I sold it.

And there before me was the glory of the God of Israel, as in the vision I had seen in the plain. (Ezekiel 8:4 NIV)

The Glory of the Lord

After selling the clinic God spoke to me and told me to rest. And for the next three years I rested focusing my energy on my children and how I could serve God by serving others. I took all five of the children on a cruise. They entertained me and encouraged me to make new friends. But out of nowhere I discovered a major problem.

I thought I had been very careful when I sold the Veterinary clinic and all the tax issues were resolved with the final documents. But I was deeply alarmed when at the end of the year my tax accountant told me that I owed $150,000 to the IRS! This was a big shock because I had included my tax accountant in every transaction from the sale. I was not prepared to pay the IRS $150,000. I didn't have that much money.

"I can't pay $150,000," I told him through my frustrated tears. "You need to search the laws to be sure. This must be a mistake."

"I don't think so, AB," My tax man told me. But he agreed to file for an extension and look deeper into my problem.

After a few weeks, I was called to his office and my accountant assured me that he had exhausted all possible ways to solve my problem and that I did owe the $150,000.

He had prepared some paperwork, requesting an additional extension. "I have the papers drawn up, AB," he told me. "Come on by and sign them and I'll mail it for you."

With the extension and interest, I now owed the IRS even more than the original $150,000. I was in despair again and all my friends were praying for me. I was so upset because I was just about to regain my economic stability and now this happened. "Father God! Where are you?" I asked.

*My tears have been my food day and night,
While they say to me all day long, "Where is
your God?" (Psalm 42:3 NASB)*

I went by the tax office and signed the papers, but unlike my usual routine I decided not to leave the paperwork for my accountant to mail. I picked up the file and slipped it into my bag. "I'll take it home and mail it myself," I told him. Looking back, I don't' know why I said that. I had always allowed my accountant to mail my documents for me.

I came home and walked into my living room removing the tax file from my bag. I sat down and I opened the

file trying to make sense of what it said I owed completely unprepared to pay this enormous amount of money.

In despair I cried out, "Lord, You were there when I
needed You. It was You who told me to sell the clinic. I
don't know what to do! I need Your help!" I tossed the
file on the table, and I didn't mail it.

> *Therefore let's approach the throne of grace*
> *with confidence, so that we may receive*
> *mercy and find grace for help at the time of*
> *our need. (Hebrews 4:16 NASB)*

And then something absolutely strange happened. I
completely forgot about it. I put the file on the coffee table, left the room and for two days I didn't think about
it, worry about it or even see it sitting there on the table.
I didn't sign the form and I forgot to mail it.

Thinking back on that time in my life over the years
I've asked myself, "How could you forget that you owe
the government $150,000?!"

I admit that it's not normal and it's very weird. But it
was of God. He completely washed it from my mind as
He worked on my tax problem for me.

On the third day, I was straightening the house, when
I realized that I had forgotten the tax forms. "Oh my! I
forgot to do this!" I exclaimed in a panic.

It was too late to mail them that afternoon and that
night I was attending a prayer meeting at a friend's house.
Before we began to pray, I told them what had happened

with my tax troubles and how in my haste to give the problem to God, I had neglected to mail the documents.

"I don't know what to do," I cried. "I'm in even more trouble now."

One of my friends at the prayer meeting had been praying about this problem since it first turned up. She hugged me and said, "I have a guy who does my taxes and he's phenomenal. Let's ask him to help." I finally agreed to have someone else look at my files and see if I really did have to pay this huge sum of money.

I went to this new tax office, gave them the files, and sat down. I could see a whole team of specialists looking over the file, researching, consulting and figuring numbers. I sat there praying in the waiting room and watching them work. I could see two people working in one office and then I could look back across to the other side of the main room where another woman was typing. I was so scared, waiting alone for the results of this last-ditch effort to save my finances. I could feel my own pulse pounding in my head and I just kept asking God to help these people find a way that I didn't owe all this money.

All of a sudden in the corner of the waiting area a soft glow began to appear. The glow became brighter and seemed to have light within light. It was swirling, extremely bright, yet soft and comforting.

The light seemed to swell and almost pulsate with my own heartbeat. There was a shape of a man seated on a high chair, his arms resting on the sides of the chair with hands reaching out. His face was shrouded in the enchanting glow. The radiance took on a round shape, and became brighter, and brighter. An overwhelming wave of holiness hit me and I rocked back as it washed over me with a tangible sensation several times.

The experience was so astounding that I don't even know how to explain what I saw, but I knew instantly that what I was seeing was the glory of the Lord. I was awestruck. The light continued to gently swirl in the corner, and I gasped at the revelation of something so holy.

The image was deeply inspiring, and I started trembling. I was so overwhelmed I didn't know what to say. I was the only one who seemed to notice this Presence because the tax accountants were still talking and working on my files.

The light was so brilliant that I covered my eyes. I couldn't believe what I was seeing yet I yearned to see it again. I peeked out from behind my hands. I knew it was real and I wanted to see it again. But about that time, the tax accounts began talking excitedly and the woman behind the computer screen said, "Good news, AB!"

I looked over at her and saw her smiling at me. "Are you ready?" she asked.

I nodded.

She turned the computer screen toward me and hit a key on the keyboard. It showed that I owed \$29,000 for federal tax and \$8000 for state.

I blinked my eyes, "Are you sure?" I asked.

"I hold a tax license," my friend smiled. "I'm sure."

"Wait a minute," I said. "I'll be right back."

I got up and raced out to the side of the parking lot where I thought no one could see me and I yelled, "Jesus! Jesus! Jesus!" I was screaming so loud and crying.

All the tax accountants who had been working on the forms could see me through the office windows and they were celebrating too.

I went back into the building and asked one more time, "Are you sure?" I was feeling confused and mixed up. "I don't mind paying half."

I looked at the woman behind the computer. She was crying too. She said, "AB, Somebody loves you. Somebody cares about you and Somebody is watching over you."

I wiped my eyes and nodded, "I know." I sniffled. "He was right there." I pointed to the corner.

"Who?" she asked.

"God," I whispered.

"You saw him?" she asked not with disbelief, but with a tone of respect and awe.

I nodded.

She smiled at me. "See what I mean? He was here! I thought so. What does he look like?"

I swallowed and thought for a moment. "Oh, there was so much glory and light. It was so bright that I couldn't see His face." I explained.

I began to tremble again as I recounted my Lord's presence. "He was sitting down with His hands like this," I extended my arms as if they were on the arms of a chair. "And there was so much glory and peace and love in this room that it didn't even matter anymore if I had to pay all that money to the IRS."

"Oh, AB," my friend laughed. "You don't owe all that money. Go home and thank Him."

I went home feeling refreshed but unsettled. I couldn't sleep. All night long my body was shaking, as I recalled that holy moment with God.

The next morning, I was supposed to do something at the church, but my body continued to shake, and I felt that I couldn't perform my tasks at church. I called my Pastor and briefly explained that I couldn't come to church that day and why.

"This is the day you must come to church!" she exclaimed. "You need to be here." And she sent someone over to get me.

When we arrived at church and walked in the foyer the very first person I saw was a woman who I knew well through a prayer group. Our group had been praying for this woman's husband who had been very ill for a long while.

I walked up to her and said, "Your husband is going to be healed."

I don't know why I told her that except that God put those words in my mind, heart, and mouth. And within a few weeks the man was healed. This incident marked the beginning of a whole new ministry for me. God began opening doors for me everywhere. I took on more of a leadership role in the church. I experienced grace in portions I had never experienced before.

For of His fullness we have all received, and grace upon grace. (John 1:16 NASB)

www.ingramcontent.com/pod-product-compliance
Lightning Source LLC
Chambersburg PA
CBHW031523120626
46545CB00005B/1967